Asia

The Book of Lights - I

UNVEILING
the MYSTERY of
GOD

Spiritual Translations by
John A. Parry

P&P
Publishing

The Book of Lights - I
Unveiling the Mystery of God
By John A. Parry

Published by:
P & P Publishing
P.O. Box 1051
Warren, Michigan, 48090 U.S.A.

Bible quotes appearing in this presentation were taken from the King James version. For purposes of clarity, the author has occasionally rephrased the wording in order to better convey his spiritual intent. Phrases in italics are the Author's comments.

Edited by Anne Daugherty
Typesetting by Diane Binder-Collins

Preassigned LCCN: 2003097884
ISBN:0-9745740-0-7

Cover design and illustration by **Lightbourne, LLC,** © 2004.

TABLE OF CONTENTS

Glossary

This glossary is provided to aid the reader in understanding materials specifically selected for this presentation.

Adept—One whose mind is in unity with the Life-Source, and who is proficient in interpreting the relationship existing between the above and the below.

End Time—The culminating of God's revelatory work. ("It is finished.")

First Judgment—The mind's awakening to the inherent unity that relates mankind to God's work.

Last Judgment—The uniting of the Spirit of God and the Spirit of man in one all-inclusive collective consciousness.

Light-pattern—The nonchanging principles embodied in Creation that characterize God, Christ and Man.

Linear—The perception that all relates to time and place, that all follows the time-line continuum.

Macrocosm—Infinitely large. A universal principle. God and his universe.

Microcosm—The infinite, *in finite*. Man as God's image and likeness. A universal simile.

Non-effect—To make void through self-exclusion or misinterpretation.

Outpictured—The transposing of Life's innate principles into formal manifestation.

Parallelism—In agreement; of one mind; comparable, as in the axiom, "Things equal to the same thing are equal to each other."

Passover—The mind's passage from a lower to a higher state of comprehension. ("I have greatly desired to eat this *Passover* with you.")

Quasi-Spiritual—God is spiritual. His works are expressions of his character; they are quasi-spiritual. All manifestation, visible and invisible, is therefore counted as quasi-spiritual.

Quicken—To give Life to what was spiritually latent or lifeless.

Regeneration—Empowering the mind to interpret the principles embodied in quasi-spiritual manifestation.

Resurrection—The raising of the quasi-spiritual mind to a Spiritual level of comprehension.

Similitude—A symbol of like nature, anything that is similar to—an image and likeness; a parable; something comparable; a simile; reflective, etc.

Spiritual Translation—To remove the time-line from interpretation and view all in the eternal now. ("I AM.")

Temporal—Formed from natural elements; of an earthy nature; sensory by design; mankind's first two levels of reality.

True Light—The inherent "Light of Life" that elevates mankind into becoming an intelligent being.

Ultimate Reality—To know God; to recognize yourself in all he has made; to live in harmony with The Eternal.

Voidal—What was, is not, and yet is. Without foundation, the "bottomless pit," to believe in error, the mind's dark misconceptions.

Way-Shower—A person who uses natural imagery to convey eternal principles; an interpreter of the Creator's work in its eternal glory.

Introduction

The Book of Lights – Unveiling the Mystery of God is consistent with John's Book of Revelation, which reads:

"I saw the dead, small and great, stand before God; and the books *of the Bible* were opened. And another book was opened, which is the book of life, T*he Book of Lights*, ("In him was Life and the Life was the Light") and the dead were judged out of those things that were written in the books, according to their works."

REVELATIONS 20:12

I n that context, this work calls upon the reader to exercise *true judgment* ("Judge not according to the appearance, but judge right judgment") to judge the mind's transcending levels of comprehension.

It is no secret that mankind's world is presently overrun with religious doctrines and spiritual misconceptions. There are hundreds of "beliefs" to choose from but none satisfy the soul's hunger for understanding life's fundamental truths. Is there anyone who has not questioned, "What am I? Where am I going? What happens to me when I die? And, why does not God come to our aid when we need his help so desperately?" These crucial questions are met with silence and simplistic answers, such as: "There are things we are not meant to know." As an alternative, all generations are asked to have faith in the unknown and to hold fast to their "beliefs."

For thousands of years, humanity has wandered in a chaotic wilderness of its own choosing. It has tried, unsuccessfully, to fit God's unity into the errors of its own divided world. As the disciple James explained, "You receive not because you ask amiss." Rather, mankind has chosen divisive "belief" and "will worship" over knowing his own image and likeness in the Creator's work. Consequently, the path to true spirituality – and, subsequently, a better world – has become the path least trodden; a path recognized only by mystics, spiritual adepts and enlightened Way-showers who too infrequently bring light into the world.

Now, after thousands of years of deprivation and conflict, we have come to that promised Age wherein the eternal character of God will be openly revealed to all mankind; a time when heaven and earth shall witness to the eternal truths that reveal the Creator's character and all that was previously clouded will emerge unfettered.

The Book of Lights – Unveiling the Mystery of God is the first of three books that progressively disclose the hidden path leading to Life's Ultimate Reality – expressed by Jesus as "The kingdom of heaven". It unfolds as a spiritual primer and continuing guide that the reader will need to refer to as their comprehension of God's eternal presence grows. It provides a door through which you may walk without being afraid of what you will find on the other side; however, you must take the first step. God does not initiate true judgment, he only responds when called upon for guidance. ("I will give to every man according to his works.")

Finally, as a precautionary warning, do not try to fit the limitations of mankind's "beliefs" into God's eternal reality. As Jesus explained:

"No man sews new cloth into an old garment; for that which is intended to patch the hole only makes it worse.

Neither do men put new wine into old skins; for when the wine expands the skins break and both the skins and the wine are lost.

But they put new wine into new skins and both expand and are preserved."

The truth this simile conveys is that we must walk away from our "earthy beliefs" before we can embrace knowledge and understanding of The Eternal. The "best wine" is, therefore, served only after the mind's first knowledge is spent. The "New Wine" is then brought forth to consummate the marriage of man's spiritual unity with The Eternal. All who attend the wedding feast and drink from this cup then rejoice.

"I AM THE WAY"
"I AM THE TRUTH"
"I AM THE LIFE"

Spiritual Translations

**"HE HAS TRANSLATED US INTO
THE KINGDOM
OF HIS BELOVED SON."**

A New Beginning

"And God said, Let there be light! And there was light. And God divided the light from the darkness."

GENESIS 1:3-4

Some fifty-plus years ago, I unexpectedly passed through an invisible curtain into a world best described as THE ULTIMATE REALITY. The experience was traumatic, one I now recognize as my personal introduction to life's transcendent truth. It was an incident that would change my perception of life forever. Unrecognized at the time, it marked the beginning of a progressive exploration into the mysteries of God.

I was raised from childhood to be a "believer" in God and I tried to practice my beliefs. But believing and practicing the rules of religion are not enough. There is a great chasm between religious belief and God's ultimate truth. In retrospect, I was a tolerant fence-sitter, a man who neither agreed – nor disagreed – with any particular form of worship. I had tried to understand the Bible's various presentations, which at the time seemed remote and unrelated to this present Age. Suddenly, without warning, my beliefs were challenged by events I could not understand, and they were collapsing under the weight of ignorance and misinformation. As a result, I found myself wandering aimlessly in "a land wherein I was a stranger."

The experience was emotionally draining. The conflicting differences between the world that pressed in upon me and the one to which I was accustomed sent my "reasonable thoughts" retreating in disarray. To relieve the mounting pressure and anxiety, I spent countless hours searching for materials that might provide insights into the events that were unfolding. Phenomenally, the books of the Bible provided numerous passages alluding to a spiritual Pass-over of consciousness, a "second appearing" of truth, a "hidden manna" which lay beneath the Word's surface. As I studied the Bible's various comparisons I felt an exchange of consciousness taking place. By exercising a system of adoption, or conversion, a union was formed between the Word and myself. Though unforeseen, this union provided the key to unlocking life's deepest mysteries.

With the multitude of religious doctrines available today it would seem plausible that at least one of them would have understood the Word's dual nature. Not so! I was told, "There are things that we are not meant to know." I was not convinced. As I later discovered, traditional religion is governed by linear thought while spiritual truth is governed by parallel thought. Traditional worship is built "precept upon precept and line upon line," while spiritual truth is built upon a concept of COMMON-UNITY. Therefore, the church of individual choice sees God's truth through a dark glass, never face-to-face.

As a simile of church tradition, the designated clergyman, serving as the Word's quasi-spiritual "Way-shower," officiates at the wedding ceremony wherein the bride and groom await being united; but the bride's veil is not removed until his ceremonial work is finished. Only then is her face unveiled for all to see. At that time, the limited scope of the cleric's ritualistic labor is made clear. The spiritual "Word of Life" that was hidden in the formal presentation is revealed and the bride's crowning glory, *the marriage of heaven and earth*, is brought to light.

Referring to this promised unveiling of quasi-spiritual truths, when Jesus taught the coming of God's kingdom to his disciples he spoke of a dimension of enlightenment they had yet to experience. He referred to his entry into this mysterious realm and how they would eventually follow him. He explained, "Where I go you cannot now come; but afterwards, *after the Son of man is glorified,* you shall follow." I searched for years but found no one who could specifically explain the mystery of Christ's coming into the kingdom of his Father. Some believed he spoke of life beyond the grave. Others said he would return at the end of the world to set up his kingdom. None answered to my satisfaction. In time, I understood what God meant when he said, "I will gather a peculiar people unto myself." For what I was seeing was, indeed, out of the ordinary.

Today, after wandering through what seemed an endless maze of religious contradiction and misinformation, I must conclude that the world's religious community has fallen upon its own sword. It is accurately described as "a house divided against itself." Where religious doctrine is concerned, nothing has changed in the last two thousand years. As Paul observed, "The whole Creation groans· and travails in pain, awaiting the glorious manifestation of the Sons of God."

My initial reaction to this dreadful situation was that although God had selectively revealed his secret to a few, he did not want his mysteries to become common knowledge. Yet that view was rebutted when Jesus said, "A light is not brought forth to be hidden under a bushel but to be set upon a lamp stand for all to see." It is common sense that when we install lights in the rooms of a house, we intend to illuminate its dark corners. There is no way to justify the mind's darkness when such great light is available. As for teaching others, I knew I could never give to another what I had not first given to myself. So, for years, I tenaciously labored "dividing the light from the darkness."

I was twenty-seven years old when I first passed beyond this mysterious curtain, and the five years that immediately followed yielded only incremental amounts of related information. However, through patience and persistence, my related knowledge eventually increased and, like a snowball rolling downhill, the weight and momentum of accelerating truth impelled me forward. To the mind's eye, these new discoveries appeared in every way as coexisting worlds, as a world existing in the midst of a world.

Make no mistake: The veil that hides God's kingdom from man's eyes cannot be removed through traditional religious instruction. Granted, there are myriad numbers of books and teachers available to those seeking peripheral information, but the knowledge of which I speak is that true and precious gift that comes to man only through the Father of lights. It is a knowledge that proceeds directly from God. As the psalmist witnessed, "Except the Lord build the house, they labor in vain that build it. Except the Lord keep the gate, the watchman awakens but in vain." In that same context, Isaiah adds: "The Lord has said, Heaven is my throne and the earth is my footstool. Where is the house that you would build in my name? Have I not fashioned my place of rest with my own hand?" The conflicting differences between God's Word and man's religious doctrines will be explained in depth as we proceed.

Like all who ponder the Bible's content, I, too, found its message difficult to understand. That is because Scripture's revelation is both symbolic and dimensional. The Word first descends into darkness, then reascends into the light. In this way its message becomes all things to all men, that by all means it may save some of them. Adding to the confusion, the exchanges between the Bible's participants are often incomplete. For instance, when God instructed Moses on how to build the tabernacle in the wilderness, he said, "Be sure to make all things according to the pattern shown to you in the mount." But exactly what that pattern was is not revealed. When David inquired of God, "What is man that you are mindful of him? And the Son of man that you visit him?" God's reply is not given. When Jesus tells the Father, "I have finished the work that you gave me to do," he does not reveal what that work entailed. Not least, when the disciples asked the risen Christ when they could expect his return and the coming end of the world, he veiled his reply, saying, "Of that day knows no man; no, not the angels of heaven, but my Father only." With such ambiguities, we are cast adrift upon an uncharted sea. But the mysteries hidden within its depths ultimately give up their secrets.

Taking all things into consideration, I saw no choice but to leave my old "beliefs" behind and begin anew. Committing myself to the unknown, I began to move on. I followed the advice given in the book of Hebrews, which reads:

> "Leaving the principles of the doctrine of Christ, let us go on to perfection; not laying again the foundation of repentance from dead works and faith toward God. Of the doctrine of baptism, and of laying on of hands, and eternal judgment. And this we will do, if God permit."

The Void

"And the earth was without form, and
void; and darkness was upon the face of
the deep. And the Spirit of God moved
upon the face of the waters."

GENESIS 1:2

The first lesson to be learned about gaining entry
into the mysterious domain of God's kingdom is
that the Creator does not impose his will upon
man. He responds to his call, but only when man's
earthy knowledge and subsequent misconceptions of
life are made void. ("I come, O Lord, to do your will.")
Importantly, in his response God gives only of what is
his; namely, himself. ("Ask anything IN MY NAME and
it shall be given to you.") By "voiding" the mind's
temporal and quasi-spiritual "beliefs," the mystery that
surrounds entry into the Father's kingdom is resolved.
("He that seeks his life must lose it; and he that would
lose his life for my sake, *for the sake of spiritual truth,*
shall find it unto life eternal.") Subsequent to recognizing this voidal state, the Spirit of truth comes in

Christ's name and begins teaching its newborn heirs as children. Incrementally, the mind's conflicting levels of comprehension are led into all truth and man's new spiritual frame is glorified with the Father's glory. ("I will not leave you comfortless. I will come to you.") The heirs of God's Spirit are thus welcomed into Life's Ultimate Reality. ("Except you become as little children, you shall not enter the kingdom of heaven.")

In regard to the world's present theological maze, the most pressing question confronting those seeking spiritual fulfillment is: "How do I obtain a voidal response?" ("You receive not because you ask amiss.") This is the most difficult of all challenges. To be honest, I discovered this secret quite by accident. I was born an idealist. I once believed the only way to be successful in life was to be honest and to work hard. I was half right, honesty is important. But the problem with work, of any kind, is that it has a tendency to assume the role of master. It is not an uncommon occurrence. It can happen to you. It happened to me, and it literally ruined any chance I had for acquiring true spirituality. By the time I was twenty-seven, my life was in shambles – at least it appeared that way to me. My world could be summed up in one word: WORK! For me, there appeared little else to live for and I saw no path for escape.

In desperation I asked God to show me if there was anything better in this world than I had known. Looking back, it appears that I had unwittingly wandered into a likeness of the dark void from which God, in his primordial beginning, had emerged. I was totally unprepared for what followed. His Spirit quickly responded! And that response completely shattered my composure. At the sound of his voice, my days as a "believer" and a "fence-sitter" abruptly ended. I had discovered, firsthand, that God listens to man and will speak to him face-to-face ... if he is honestly willing to listen. ("They shall see his face, and his name shall be written in their foreheads.")

While the idea of man entering and then exiting from a voidal life may come as a surprise to many, it nevertheless stands as the FIRST PRINCIPLE in resolving one of life's deepest mysteries. It discloses the paralleling path man must follow in passing from quasi-spiritual to spiritual understanding. As it was in the beginning, when the Creator emerged from the primordial void and beheld his "true light," man must also emerge from his voidal misconceptions and behold his "true light." ("I do only those things I see with the Father.") Thereafter, his eternal glory will shine forth. Scripture expresses this regenerative experience as Christ's promised return, his Second Coming – or, as expressed in this presentation, the Word's second reading. It is a revelatory experience wherein all the holy angels descend from on high to witness to God's presence. ("Let all the angels of God, *all the truths of God*, witness to him.") With understanding of the Most High imparted to the psyche, man is then translated into the kingdom of heaven. ("I have greatly desired to eat this Passover with you.")

With the mind's passage from dark misconceptions into patterns of spiritual light, additional credence is given to the Word's power to deliver man from his voidal state. Reformation through "the renewing of the mind" thus emerges as THE SECOND PRINCIPLE of God; a regenerative precept that is endemic to the Creator's character. This second principle is demonstrated when Creation's radiant light, *the Christ*, speaks to Moses from the midst of Sinai's fiery bush, declaring, "I AM that I AM." Upon coming face-to-face with the Infinite in finite, life as Moses had known it was made void. His eyes were opened and spiritual renewal rushed in to direct his future.

In reference to events pertaining to Creation's primordial beginning, when the principle of renewal was sown into God's manifesting light, all assumed the character of an evolving work, a work presently defined by the scientific community as "the time-space continuum." In relationship to our present discussion, it corresponds to Creation's linear and parallel appearance. In like manner, it applies to humanity's perception of life and death. In correlating this inverse relationship, Scripture reports, "It is given unto all men once to die," *to experience darkness before obtaining the light of spiritual judgment,* which tells us that that God is using temporal death as a vehicle for advancing the spiritual aspect of his work. In this even Christ, himself, was not exempt, as witnessed by the dark cloud that hid his true character from mankind's view until the time of the Word's reformation.

Because Creation's first judgment was based upon linear progression, not until its quasi-spiritual light-patterns obtained an inverse witness – a witness similar to that of their Creator – could an all-inclusive judgment be achieved. It was, therefore, expedient to provide those patterns with an "in-version" of their own character. Creation's ever-changing appearance could then be reconciled to its never-changing Source. ("Two *parallel* witnesses fulfill the law of Life.") With that accomplished, all would converge to form A UNIFIED COLLECTIVE CONSCIOUSNESS.

To facilitate that endeavor, man was fashioned as God's chosen vehicle to reverse the outward flow of his linear work; however, the linear perceptions of man's mind would prevent him from immediately recognizing the inverse nature of his calling. As a result, his thoughts would languish in a state of temporal somnolence for thousands of years. When the "end time" of this reconciling venture had finally arrived, Christ would affirm, "Father, I have finished the work you gave me to do. Now I come to you." With the quickening of the labors identified with that era, an all-inclusive judgment would be attained. The Spirit of truth would descend from on high and man would assume his role as the Creator's judgmental centerpiece. As the Bible relates, "He shall not rest or be discouraged until he has set judgment in the earth." As a prelude to mankind receiving this precious gift, Christ explained, "Where I go you cannot now come, but afterwards you shall follow. It is my Father's good pleasure to give you his kingdom." And what he promised was quickly fulfilled. True Self-judgment thus emerged as THE THIRD PRINCIPLE of God.

In taking an overview of man's judgmental role, we find that in the primordial beginning there were two basic factors to be addressed: one of Causal Spirit, the other of a dark void. Therefore, in preparing man for his forthcoming venture, two forms of judgment had to be instated. The first judgment would relate to mankind characterizing the elements of outer darkness, the second judgment would relate to his characterizing the internal glory embodied in the Creator's work.

Scripture refers to these two forms of judgment as the first and last judgments.

In man, the first judgment, *his first understanding of life,* is indicative of knowledge obtained from temporal sources. The last judgment, *his second understanding of life,* is indicative of knowledge obtained from spiritual sources. Comparably, his first judgment is given to voidal darkness and signifies death. His last judgment is given to the "true light" that resides within God's Spirit and signifies life eternal. Because these two judgments were historically embodied, *typically through mirrored similes,* each judgment emerged having life within itself. With darkness and light now witnessing side by side, the specter of rotating cycles of life and death had a dire affect upon the psyche. Because man lived on a temporal level of cognizance, he completely failed to understand that death and life were to be experienced as "living states" – that through inverse evolution, he was destined to pass first from life unto death, then from death unto L*ife!*

Contrary to religious belief, then, man's death and resurrection are not events relating to the distant future. Conversely, they are a very important part of his evolving experience. It is the raising of thought from a voidal reality to a spiritual reality. Identifying himself as the Word of Life that provided the mind with spiritual renewal, Christ explained, "I am the resurrection and the Life, *the light of spiritual understanding.* He that comes to me, though he were dead, *held captive by dark misconceptions,* yet shall he live." We thus see THE THREE BASIC PRINCIPLES OF GOD – *voidal darkness, spiritual renewal and true self-judgment* – emerging as primary factors in obtaining Life's Ultimate Reality.

We are, therefore, confronted with the challenge of knowing ourselves in the void, even as God first knew himself in the void. Having made that descent and having recognized its end, spiritual renewal quickly follows. ("Behold, I come quickly.") Through this regenerative experience, the mind's quasi-spiritual error is removed and man's promised resurrection is fulfilled. ("He that overcomes shall inherit all things.")

In keeping with the concept of Spirit emerging from the void, the Bible provides two readings, each of which the reader should be eminently aware. Again, these two presentations constitute the first and last judgments. The Word's first reading is linear and relates to the voidal aspect of the time-space continuum. Its second reading is a parallelism, or simile, and relates to the "true light" that emerged from the void. Because both readings are embodied in one presentation, the first reading, *the linear Word made flesh,* must suffer death. Thereafter, the light of eternal truth within the Word's second reading shines forth. ("A testimony is of non-effect until after the death of the testator.") Christ therefore told his disciples, "It is expedient for you that I go away, *for the disciples initially interpreted Christ's words on a quasi-spiritual level, the first judgment.* But if I go away I will come again to receive you unto myself, *his promised spiritual return; or the last judgment,* that where I am there you may be also." We thus see God meeting man in the voidal segment of his work and then translating him into the eternal truth that appears within the Word's second reading. ("He has translated us into the kingdom of his beloved Son.")

Having experienced the conflicting ways of the temporal mind, we all know that living in the void is not easy. And, reflective of life's temporal complexities, extricating ourselves from voidal captivity is an enormous challenge. But we are not left without resources. God has prepared a second reading of his Word – "The Arm of the Lord" – to accomplish our renewal. But our spiritual quickening is conditional: "He that seeks his life must lose it!" This is accomplished by exercising "The Spirit of Adoption!" The Bible holds no greater secret than this: To gain entrance to the kingdom of God, you must adopt his Word! That translates to: THINK PARALLEL! Christ exercised the tenet of adoption when he said, "All that the Father has are mine and all mine are the Father's." If you adopt the Word, the Word will adopt you. But if you deny the Word, the Word will deny you. ("If you confess me, *the true light that is in you*, before men, I will confess you before my Father and his angels. But if you deny me, *the true light that is in you*, before men, I will deny you before my Father and his angels.")

The tenet of adoption, which directs us to flood the dark void within ourselves with God's "true light," brings us full circle in probing the void's mystery. It calls upon us to reflect upon our chaotic state of mind and to compare what we see with that primal condition wherein God's voice was first heard crying out from the abyss, "Let there be light!" But, until that act of contrition is performed, our spiritual renewal is held in abeyance.

3

The First Man

"And God said, Let the waters under the heaven be gathered together unto one place and let the dry land appear. And God called the dry land Earth; and the gathering together of the waters called he Seas."

GENESIS 1:9-10

It is no secret that Creation is long on chaos and short on tranquility. Scientific exploration has confirmed that the universe is violent. Consequently, the transposing of God's primal orientation into visible light was successful only in part. It provided a reflective picture of the Creator's voidal state, but it outwardly revealed nothing concerning his innate character. He was, therefore, limited to judging his work by "outer appearance," as opposed to "true self judgment." It thus behooved God to create a vehicle wherein an all-inclusive judgment could be achieved. That choice was revealed when God addressed his light-pattern, saying, "Let us make man in our image and after our likeness." That is, let Creation's light-pattern, *his Christ,* which reflects the Principal that emerged from the void, *the*

Father, appear in the person of "Adam." So, by design, man was made in the image and likeness of that quickening union that preceded him.

When the Creator fashioned Adam as a vehicle to expedite "true judgment," man inherited two natures. Formed of the dust of the ground, he was first of the earth – earthy. And when God breathed the breath of Life into his nostrils, man became a microcosm of all things preceding him. Therein he was characterized as "Human Nature," a reflective entity capable of expressing the Creator's temporal and spiritual attributes. He thus became the potential benefactor of all things in heaven and on earth. ("Therefore, let no man glory in men; for all things are yours.")

However, in studying God's intent, we find a significant problem arose when he imparted his image and likeness to Adam. Whereas in the beginning Creation had evolved outward, progressing from Spirit into form, in Adam all now evolved inward, progressing from form into Spirit. To achieve this inversion of substance, Adam's body was fashioned as a sensory vehicle – a mechanism that provided the Creator with a method of changing visible Creation into invisible form. Thus, in Adam, God's work was passed from temporal evolution to temporal involution. Man's spiritual evolution still remained far off. Nonetheless, the Creator's work had acquired an inverse dimension and man emerged as the Creator's all-inclusive "living life"; a vehicle capable of assessing and judging all things. Jesus referred to this gift when he told his followers: "All power is given to me in heaven and earth. What you bind on earth shall be bound in heaven and what you release on earth shall be released in heaven."

Because "two witnesses" were needed to rightly judge Creation's diverse aspects, we read: "And God said, It is not good that the man should be alone. Let us make one who will conceive from him and help meet his needs." Accordingly, Eve – *the mind* – was fashioned from the flesh of Adam's flesh and the bone of Adam's bone and, as such, became a living extension of Adam's sensory body. Characterized as "two in one body" but appearing separately, the first couple was thus counted as one flesh, providing the Creator and his outpictured light-pattern with a temporal version of their linear self. As Genesis relates, "Male and female created he them." Therein, Adam and Eve were placed in Creation's Garden of God as co-inhabiters.

Noting that God formed Adam before Eve, *the need for the body to precede the mind,* accounts for the sequence of events that followed. Since Adam's body was designed as a sensory vehicle, it followed that the mind, Eve, was limited to sensory cognizance. Consequently, the two were deprived of spiritual judgment. To bring those inherent limitations to light, we find the analogy of Eve being confronted by the serpent, *the faculty of sensory Reason,* that was hiding in Eden's Tree of Knowledge of good and evil, the tree of which God had warned: "You shall not eat the fruit thereof or you shall surely die." But the serpent *reasoned* with Eve and convinced her of the advantage to be gained by becoming a sensory god. Temporal Reason, *the serpent,* thus beguiled Eve, *the mind,* and she took his advice. She ate of the forbidden fruit and, as a result, God's spiritual counsel was made void. The stage was thus set for their expulsion from Eden's quasi-spiritual setting. When Eve, *the mind,* gave Adam, *the body,* his share of the forbidden fruit, the two began judging Creation by its appearance and their fate was sealed. They were driven from Eden into the dark concepts conceived from the outer world. Having made their spiritual inheritance "void," the earth then became their temporal home.

The chaos that surfaced with their error is emphasized when God tells Adam: "I have cursed the ground for your sake, *I have made the ground void of spiritual content for your sake.* Thorns and thistles shall it bring forth to you. You shall eat bread in the sweat of your face until you return to the ground out of which you were formed. For that formed of the dust must return to the dust, *that formed in the void must return to the void.*" Adam and Eve were thus confronted with the harsh realities of an external existence: A life that excluded knowing the "true light" God had given them for an eternal heritage.

Since humanity's present concept of life and death is totally inaccurate, it would be enlightening to review the spiritual definition of death. This is described in the following:

- Death is the absence of understanding the human frame and its relationship to the "Tree of Life."
- Death is the substituting of temporal knowledge for spiritual understanding.
- Death is the inability of the natural senses to relate to the "true light" within God's work.
- Death is the pursuit of an abstract existence.

Relating to the above, "It is given to all men once to die," *to relate only to the temporal world.* Therefore, until the mind awakens to its "true light," death prevails within the psyche as an ongoing state of reality. As the psalmist pleaded: "Hear me, O Lord. Give light to my eyes, lest I sleep the sleep of *temporal* death."

There is also a misconception regarding the doctrine of life eternal. Remember, all God has outpictured into Creation belongs to the time-space continuum. Because that continuum is relative and subject to change, it has a beginning and an end. Conversely, life eternal resides in the Spirit of God. To have understanding of the light within his Spirit is to have life eternal. This higher reality is recognized as follows:

- ○ He that communicates with God in Spirit and in truth has life eternal.
- ○ He that becomes one with the "true light" within himself has life eternal.
- ○ He that relates to the "I" in the Spirit of God ("I AM that I AM") has life eternal.
- ○ He that becomes one with the Life in all that God has made has life eternal.

Life eternal is thus recognized as the mind's Ultimate Reality; the ability to understand and experience all that is eternally true.

With Adam's exodus from Eden into the outside world, the problem confronting the Creator was how to reconcile man's voidal knowledge to his "true light." This involved revealing the primordial truth that external darkness preceded the dawn of Creation's first light. Since all that related to Creation and man now witnessed to God's voidal experience, only by exercising the principle of renewal, *the flooding of Creation's "voidal form" with the light of Life*, could the "true light" within his work shine forth. This is emphasized when God says, "Now lest the man put forth his hand and eat of the Tree of Life and live forever." Paul embraced this regenerative principle when he wrote, "He has made his light, *in man*, to shine out of darkness, *to emerge from the void*." Adam thus inherited the Creator's primal image and likeness and, as it was with God when his light emerged from the dark void, so would it be with man.

In drawing attention to the light in man that shines in a dark place, we should understand that since the void signified death, God was about to use death to overcome him that had the power of death namely, sensory Reason. The Bible uses similes to depict this "end time" and the reconciling of death. Here are a few examples:

- "I shall raise up the waste places and cause the desert to blossom as a rose."
- "I am the voice of one crying in the wilderness, make straight the crooked places; prepare a highway in the desert for our God."
- "Sing O barren, you that did not bear. Break forth into singing and cry aloud, you that did not travail with child. For more are the children of the desolate than of the married wife."
- "As long as the land lay desolate she kept Sabbath."
- "He that would come after me, let him first deny himself and take up his cross and follow me."

Voidal death became a primary factor in introducing man to the principle of spiritual renewal. It was the principle the Father chose in reconciling all things unto himself; it was also the principle Christ chose in reconciling all things unto himself. And it would be the principle mankind would be called upon to choose in reconciling all things unto himself. By causing all that God had made to share a common "end," *a common death*, all would be passed from death unto Life.

To provide for that "end," a second Adam had to appear, a spiritual Adam wherein the "all" in all of God's Spirit could judge and be judged. As we might expect, when that "second man" was finally revealed he, too, would appear in the image and likeness of all things preceding him.

"And God saw that there was no *spiritual* man to declare his truth, and he wondered that there was no intercessor. Therefore, his own Arm, *his own light*, brought salvation to him."

Mankind was thus introduced to an entirely new level of spiritual instruction – one that appeared, *in historical form*, as quasi-spiritual "signs and wonders." As time progressed, Moses and the prophets would identify those symbolic presentations as the Son of man's presence within the Creator's work. However, mankind would not be introduced to those reconciling similes until the day when God called to Abraham, saying: "Go out from the land wherein you now dwell. From your kindred and from your father's house, to a land that I will show you; and I will make of you a great nation." From that day forward, Abraham's temporal life would be made "void." He would respond to the Father's call, and thereafter he would be blessed in all God had made.

Man and His Symbolism

"Now learn the parable of the fig tree.
When its branch comes to life, and the
new leaves appear, you know that
summer is near. Likewise, when you see
the things that I show you, know that the
end is near, even at the doors."

MATTHEW 24:32-33

To reconcile four entities having diverse appearances, *the two natures of God in Creation and the two natures of God in man,* required the discovery of a "common denominator"; a vehicle that could at the same time be both visible and invisible, and could simultaneously relate to both the time-space continuum and the eternal Spirit of God. It required an entity that had the capacity to touch all things, to know all things, to judge all things and to become all things. But where could such an entity be found? The Bible provides insights into that discovery when it says, "Behold, I send my messenger before your face." "He rides upon the wings of the wind." "He thunders marvelously." Each is an aphorism alluding to a common faculty: THE WORD OF SPEECH!

To grasp the depth and importance of this disclosure, we must look beyond the outer appearance of this communicative instrument. When we probe into its symbolic foundation, we are greeted with some startling considerations. The Word's symbolic lineage, *which was formed with man in God's image and likeness,* can be traced as follows:

- In relation to man's identity, if KNOWLEDGE were removed from the mind, THE INTELLIGENT SELF WOULD CEASE TO EXIST. The physical body, sustained by a system of its own, would live on, but it would live unto itself.
- Since all knowledge is made up of individual WORD SYMBOLS, if these word symbols were removed from the mind, THE INTELLIGENT SELF WOULD CEASE TO EXIST.
- Because all word symbols are comprised of LETTER SYMBOLS and NUMERICAL SYMBOLS, if these symbols were removed from the mind, THE INTELLIGENT SELF WOULD CEASE TO EXIST.
- Ultimately, there are twenty-six letters in the English alphabet and ten symbols comprising numerology – a total of THIRTY-SIX SYMBOLS. If these basic symbols were removed from the mind, THE INTELLIGENT SELF WOULD CEASE TO EXIST.

We therefore conclude that man's entire character, his knowledge and the symbols that comprise his reality, can be reduced to THIRTY-SIX SYMBOLS. These thirty-six figures embrace all of Creation's knowledge and emerge within man as God's living Word.

When this living symbolism is translated into terms of productivity, it becomes clear that all man attributes to his genius rests squarely upon the base of these thirty-six signs. How his mind arranges and interprets their patterns determines all. ("All things were made by him, *God's living Word*, and without him was not anything made that was made.")

In keeping with this analysis, the audible word emerges as a symbolic expression of the thought that formed it. And, in a comparable way, the multitudes of visible structures formed by man's intellect are recognized as the visible presence of an invisible intelligence. But what we discover within these parameters is that the mind only reflects what appears on a grander scale: namely, Creation appearing as a symbolic replica of its Creator and Adam appearing as a symbolic replica of all that preceded him. It is not surprising, then, that the book of Hebrews affirms, "Things are not made by things that do appear." Knowing the Jews were unaware God had woven his Word into their identity, *as a twofold parallelism,* Christ warned, "Judge not according to the appearance, but judge right judgment."

John underscored the importance of mankind understanding his relationship to the Word and the correlative principle that enjoined him to all things when he wrote: "In the beginning was the Word, and the Word was with God, and the Word was God. The same, *all-inclusive relationship,* was in the beginning with God." As demonstrated in the correlation between speech and thought, the "Word" is *with* the "thought" and the "Word" *is* the "thought." The same was in the beginning with the thought. In turn, the "thought," *the intelligent light,* is *with* the Life and the "thought" *is* the intelligent Life. Christ referred to this alliance when he told his followers, "The words that I speak are Spirit; and they are Life."

Elaborating on this parallelism, the disciple continues, "In him, *in God's Word,* was Life; and THE LIFE WAS THE LIGHT OF MEN, and the light shines in *temporal* darkness and the darkness comprehends it not." John thus determines that the "light of Life" within man, the "light of Life" within Creation and the "light of Life" within the Father are one and the same. Herein, the Word that was made flesh in Jesus Christ is identified as the fruition of that image and likeness that was introduced, as "man," some four thousand years earlier, when Adam was first brought into the world. John confirms this truth when he adds, "This is the true light that lights every man coming into the world." The disciple thus recognized man as "God's living Word," an entity comparable to the light that emerged from the void at Creation's primordial inception.

In drawing attention to the structural unity that joins man to God and Christ, we should consider the inherent division that separates temporal man from spiritual man. While temporal man is essentially sensory and lives unto himself, spiritual man lives by virtue of the light that God's Spirit has vested in him. ("Of myself I can do nothing. It is the Father within me that does the work.") Because temporal thought is externalized and judges by sensory appearance, it remains void of all understanding pertaining to spiritual truth. Residing as "a law unto itself," it is counted as spiritually dead. On the other hand, having "the light of Life" within itself, spiritual thought forever flourishes. ("As the Father has life in himself, so has he given to the Son to have life in himself; and he has given him authority to execute judgment.") We thus see two distinct forms of reality emerging in man: a first reality, which is temporal and characterized as "of the earth, earthy"; and a second reality, which is spiritual and characterized as "the Lord from heaven." ("The first man is of the earth, earthy. The second man is the Lord from heaven.")

Accordingly, through the Word's transcending power, man evolves from temporal darkness into spiritual light. Through conversion of the mind's symbolism, man is raised from an earthy state to a heavenly state and, therein, is passed from death unto Life. ("He that believes in me, though he were dead, yet shall he live.") In keeping with this newness of Life, man relinquishes his old name, his temporal identity, and receives a new name, a spiritual identity. A simile of this exchanging of names is re-enacted at traditional weddings when the bride gives up her maiden name to assume her husband's name, signifying their combined spiritual unity. When the veil hiding the bride's face is removed, the spiritual image and likeness that unites the two then becomes one flesh in the eyes of God. Thereafter, they come in the name of the Lord. ("What God has joined together, let no man put asunder.") Through this symbolic re-enactment, Christ's promised return is witnessed, and the bride and groom attain God's glory, as promised. ("I will come again and receive you unto myself.")

In transposing the mystery of how the mind is spiritualized, the first thing to remember is that all form exists as quickened symbolism, and all witnesses to God's Spirit. Consequently, the key to "rebirth" is based upon converting the Word's temporal comparisons into spiritual comparisons. Since all our knowledge is comprised of symbolism and because the mind's reality is determined by the light the symbolism conveys, we have only to reinterpret the symbolism to change the character of the knowledge. This, in turn, changes the character of the man. ("Be transformed by the renewing of your mind," *by spiritually renewing the mind's symbolism.*)

Evidence clearly shows that all three of God's outpictured works – Christ's appearing within temporal Creation, Christ's appearing within temporal man and Christ's appearing as the spiritual Son of man – are symbolically related. Since "the tree is known by its fruit," all that appears within the universe – visible or invisible – must be interpreted as quickened symbolism. The Bible speaks of the "true light" within these three outpictured works as "the secret dwelling place of the Most High"; the glory into which the Creator entered on the seventh day. Solomon's *Song of Songs* refers to God's presence in the midst of his creative work when the author writes: "He that walks within the garden speaks; and his companions listen for his voice. Cause me to hear it."

Because symbolic imagery is intrinsic to man, we find his mind endowed with the power to enter or exit the time-space continuum. Having the Creator's attributes, his thoughts have the power to touch all things, to know all things and to judge all things; to be absorbed by time or to be freed from time. ("He that overcomes shall inherit all things.") But before access to these wonders can be ours we must understand our own truth. We must know ourselves in the principles extended to us when we were fashioned. Only then will we find peace.

When we measure time from the days of Adam to this present generation, we find that man has been spiritually exiled from God's presence for six thousand-plus years. To a great extent, his temporal captivity has been self-imposed. Spiritually, man has been shown much but has understood little. His loss continues. Perhaps some consolation can be drawn from Paul's lament: "Though we deny him, *though we deny the mind's true light,* yet he abides faithful. He cannot deny himself." But it is difficult to justify darkness when God's light is so abundant.

5

Two Witnesses

"And God divided the waters, *the pattern of light*, under the heaven from the waters, *the pattern of light*, above the heaven: and it was so. And the evening and the morning were the second day."

GENESIS 1:7-8

O ne of the most obvious misconceptions of Judeo-Christian theology is belief in the analogy of Moses, that Adam was created perfect and remained that way until Eve encountered the serpent in the Tree of Knowledge of good and evil. But if Adam was created perfect, the question should be asked: How could a perfect man become involved in an imperfect act? Furthermore, if God's Paradise Garden was perfect, what was the Tree of Knowledge of good and evil – and the wily serpent that made God's Word void – doing there? Clearly, Eden's parable disputes the theological assumption that Adam was originally perfect and that, through transgression, he fell into imperfection.

Realistically, as an earthy replica of God's temporal work, Adam could only be as perfect as the ground out of which he was formed. ("Let the earth bring forth after its own kind.") His ascent into God's presence, *the mind's Ultimate Reality,* was placed in abeyance when he refused God's warning and followed the serpent's deceptive advice. From the standpoint of judgment, the importance of the parable of the forbidden fruit is that it draws attention to two forms of judgment: the first, a judgment that led to "death"; the second, a judgment that led to Life.

With the emerging of these two forms of judgment, *Creation's "two great lights,"* two forms of reality became available to man. The first reality was based upon temporal knowledge, the Tree of Knowledge of good and evil. The second reality was based upon spiritual knowledge, the Tree of Life. These two forms of understanding were radically different. Whereas the first reality was based upon linear judgment, the second reality was based upon parallel judgment. Because of their conflicting differences, each judgment provided an alternative reality and each assumed its own mantle of authority. These two levels of thought are presently identified as the first and last judgments.

It is no secret that today's world is awash in judgmental conflict. Unquestionably, without linear Reason modern society would collapse. Consider the following:

- We recognize time and place, the time-space continuum, as linear.
- We recognize humanity's progress in knowledge and understanding as linear.
- We recognize the letters of the alphabet and the figures of numerology as linear.

○ We recognize the days and months and seasons of the year as linear.
○ We recognize our progress in scientific discovery as linear.
○ We recognize the evolution of the species as linear.
○ We recognize the evolving of Spirit into form, and form into Spirit, as linear.

In keeping with this rationale, the faculty of Reason assumes all responsibility for the further development of linear thought. On its assumed authority, Reason takes knowledge from the past and present and determines man's future. Linear Reason thus bears a dubious title: THE PRINCE OF THIS WORLD! THE PRINCE OF DARKNESS!

Having identified temporal Reason as man's contentious adversary, *symbolically expressed as the serpent lurking in Eden's Tree of Knowledge of good and evil,* we are now prepared to consider God's provision for overcoming this deceptive foe. It is obvious that depending on linear thought is not the answer. Beginning with Eve, what seemed reasonable to the temporal mind had been weighed in the balance and found wanting. An instrument that could circumvent this cunning power was needed. This dilemma is resolved when the mind is "converted" from linear to parallel thought. Here, a second form of judgment is acquired. The mind ascends into higher levels of understanding, *is "born again,"* and Scripture's promised "last judgment" comes to fruition.

Man's inherent ability to relate to parallel thought first appeared when Adam and Eve were formed in God's image and likeness. Had the first couple been fashioned without a reflective counterpart, they would have no base from which to judge. Consequently, man would be like the beast – without true judgment. The body was therefore provided with "two witnesses," each witness having its own reflective counterpart. In temporal man, this reflective entity is identified as sensory Reason – which, through the body's faculties, reflects on things seen. In spiritual man, this counterpart appears as God himself – which, through his Spirit, reflects on things unseen. Regarding man's calling in the Most High, the psalmist reports, "The stone that the builders refused, *the theological rejection of man's equality with God,* has become the headstone of the corner." Paul adds to the psalmist's assessment, saying, "They could not enter into the Father's glory because of unbelief!" However, once the mind's ability to spiritually convert is understood, we have only to actively embrace its truth to gain entrance to the kingdom of heaven.

The principle of "paralleling" as a way to enlighten the mind is illustrated in the following:

- Reflecting parallel thought, "Enoch walked with God and was not; for God took him."
- Reflecting parallel thought, Ruth said, "Wherever you go, I will go; and wherever you stay, I will stay. Your people shall be my people and your God shall be my God."
- Reflecting parallel thought, the psalmist exclaimed, "Look! In the volume of the book it is written of me: I come O Lord to do your will."
- Reflecting parallel thought, the Lord told Zachariah, "If you keep my ways you shall judge

my house; and I will give you places to walk among these that stand by."

- ○ Reflecting parallel thought, Isaiah wrote, "He shall grow up before the Most High as a tender plant and as a root out of a dry ground."
- ○ Reflecting parallel thought, the Father instructed the Son, "Come, sit at my right hand while I make your enemies your footstool."
- ○ Reflecting parallel thought, Jesus said, "All that the Father has are mine; and all mine are the Father's."

In walking with God, Christ displayed the perfection that was available to man through parallel thought. The depth of his unity with the Father is emphasized when the disciple, Matthew, relates, "Jesus spoke in parables, *COM-PARABLES or PARALLELS*, and without a parable spoke he not unto them."

The mind's symbolic Word is thus recognized as having a twofold nature. In like manner, the Bible's Word is revealed as having a first and second reading. While the first reading provides the mind with a linear reality, the second reading, referred to as "the hidden manna," provides the mind with a spiritual reality. When outpictured, the first reading is characterized in secular worship. In the second reading Christ appears in Spirit and in truth, receiving man unto himself.

It is no secret that we become like the level of thought we associate with. What we sow in a linear fashion we reap in a linear fashion, and what we sow in a parallel fashion we reap in a parallel fashion. Born of a mortal nature, we have all planted seeds relating to our mortality, and we have reaped a mortal harvest.

But as the apostle explained, "This mortal must put on immortality, this corrupt must put on incorruption." Renewing the mind's perception of life may be difficult, but to become truly spiritual there is no alternative. We must listen to the Word's spiritual instruction and act upon it!

Some four thousand years ago, the prophet Isaiah tried to convince Israel that God had prepared a "new covenant" for his people; a spiritual covenant. He tried to arouse them from their linear complacency, saying: "Awake! You that sleep in the dust, and the Lord shall give you light." History's record is clear. They did not listen. Traditionally, all things remain the same. Israel still awaits the coming of the Messiah; Christianity awaits his return. Yet, Christ warned: "You shall not see me from henceforth; until the day when you say, Blessed is he that comes in the name of the Lord." *Blessed is he that walks in unison with God.*

The Redeeming Light

"The Arm of the Lord, *the Word's 'true light,'* has neither form nor comeliness; and when we shall see him, there is no beauty that we should desire him."

ISAIAH 53:1-2

If the average person was asked to define God they would probably reply, "God is a Spirit." Although that brief response would not be untrue, it would provide nothing to enhance our understanding of his character. Because the substance of Spirit is nebulous, it can be recognized only through the inherent principles, which give it visibility. Those principles are found in the Creator's work. Just as "the tree is known by its fruit," so the character of the seen reveals the character of the unseen. Therefore, to unravel the mystery of God we must examine the nature of the fruit for the seed of Life is hidden within the fruit.

One of the things we discover in probing Creation's depths is that nothing, visible or invisible, stands alone – not even God himself. This is demonstrated when God is defined as "a Spirit having Life within himself." In that brief analysis we progressively pass from God, to Spirit, to Life. But this forward movement is only the beginning of a continuous trend. Recognizably, to have Life you must have expression, and that expressed by Life appears as its light. ("In him was Life, and the Life was the light.") Thereafter, the light of Life appears as the common denominator of all that exists. As John relates, "All things were made by him, *the light,* and without him was not anything made that was made." This explains, in part, the conversion that took place in the beginning when God said, "Let there be light!" With that command, Life's invisible light was outpictured into visible manifestation. The "light of Life," *Christ,* was thus "formalized" and the invisible Spirit of God was made manifest.

With the characterizing of his image and likeness within his work, Creation's radiant light became God's judgmental instrument. Having no witness of its own, however, the light could reflect only upon Creation's appearance. To judge its own character, it needed a "second witness" – an interpreter who could provide an in-depth overview of its true status. To that end, sensory Adam was fashioned. We therefore read, "Let us make man in our image and after our likeness." Designed to witness Creation's "true light," Adam was then placed in Eden, where he assumed the role of temporal interpreter and spiritual revelator.

Since God had committed all judgment to his light, when Creation's light-pattern was extended to Adam, man inherited the potential for assuming all knowledge and authority. As the recipient of all things preceding him, Adam then became equal, in microcosm, to the Creator and his Creation – the living voice of all that was made, God's living Word. Sequentially, Adam's knowledge signified Christ's light, Christ's light signified Creation's Life, and Creation's Life signified the Spirit of God.

But, when sensory Reason replaced God's counsel and authority, the first couple succumbed to temporal thought and they failed spiritually. Therefore, a second man had to be fashioned, and the Son of man, as a Christ type, emerged to provide an all-inclusive level of knowledge for the Creator and his manifesting light-patterns. Christ's testimony, *the Word's testimony,* was therefore expressed as the revelation God gave to him to show to his witnessing servants the truth and unity that was present in all he had made. The mission delegated to the Son of man was thus made clear: His work was to seek and to save that which was lost through temporal and quasi-spiritual misinterpretation! This was the labor Christ referred to when he said, "Father, I have finished the work you gave me to do."

In keeping with this effort, the Son of man identified himself with the Father's revelatory intent in a fourfold manner:

- He spoke with authority concerning God's "true light."
- He spoke with authority concerning Creation's "true light."
- He spoke with authority concerning man's "true light."
- He spoke with authority concerning the Word's "true light."

Having fulfilled the "end time" of God's reconciling work, John's Book of Revelation refers to the Son of man's ascent and return to the Father as the beginning of an all-inclusive spiritual unity; as a City of God descending from heaven, having four equal sides with a gate of entry on each side.

In relating the mind's symbolic Word to Christ's light, it will help tremendously to remember that the Word is *with* the light and the Word *is* the light. The Word-body of Christ is symbolically outpicturing four dimensions of light simultaneously: His light within the Father, his light within Creation, his light within God's "signs and wonders," and his light within man. Confusion over the Word's fourfold revelation is quickly resolved once this connection is made. Consider the following:

- "As a light, *as lightning, or enlightenment,* that comes out of the east and shines to the west, so shall be the coming of the Son of man, *the second coming of God's Word.*"
- "Before Abraham was, I, *the light,* am. Abraham rejoiced to see my day, *my truth,* and when he saw it he was glad."
- "He has delivered my soul, *my life,* from death and my feet, *my understanding,* from falling. He has called me, *his Word,* to walk before him in the light of the living."
- "The Word of the Lord is a fountain of life; and in its light we shall see light."
- "He has set judgment in his Word; and given it for a light to the people."

Having identified Christ as the Creator's characterizing light, it follows that he that has seen his light-pattern has seen the Father. ("He that has seen me has seen the Father.")

Remembering that all is "a work in progress," we should endeavor to understand the difference between temporal man and the Son of man. Because man's level of knowledge determines his level of reality, a raising of knowledge from temporal to spiritual understanding is crucial. Whereas, in the body of Adam, the seen – *visible Creation* – was translated through the senses into the unseen – *the mind of Eve* – in the Word-body of Christ, *the seen* – appearing externally as quasi-spiritual "signs and wonders," was translated into the unseen through the Word's second reading, "the mind of Christ." This transposing of the temporal mind into a higher level of reality is conveyed as a simile when Israel leaves *temporal* Egypt and passes through the divided sea on dry land. It is again expressed when they leave Sinai's *temporal* desert and pass over Jordan on *quasi-spiritual* stepping stones that were placed in the midst of the river's halted flow. These two metaphors will be discussed at length in a later chapter.

One of the great marvels of God's outpictured symbolism is that it repeatedly uses darkness, both in heaven and earth, to witness to his light. While we are inclined to think of heaven's angels as puritanical entities, the Creator makes no such distinction. On the contrary, upon bringing his light into the world he said, "Let ALL THE ANGELS OF GOD witness to him." Jesus taught the same when he said: "Bless them that curse you, do good to them that despitefully use you and persecute you; that you may be the children, *equal to the angels,* of your Father in heaven. For he makes his sun to rise on the good and the evil, and he sends his rain upon the just and the unjust." Briefly, BLESS AND CURSE NOT!

This is not to say all is well with the world. It merely returns us to the principle exercised in the beginning, when God caused his light to shine out of darkness. It is important to remember that our measure of light is directly related to our measure of darkness. Knowing this, God consigned his work to darkness, making all things void, to the end that his "true light" might shine forth. We must do likewise. ("The things that I do you shall do also.")

This brings us to theology's ongoing predicament: The fact that when Christ's redeeming light is replaced by will worship, the Word of God is made of non-effect. Christ confirmed the presence of this "stumbling stone and rock of offense" when he scolded the Jewish clergy, "You fail to enter the kingdom of God yourselves and prevent those who would enter." He again referred to theological betrayal when he informed his disciples, "He that eats bread with me has lifted up his heel against me." Some six hundred years earlier, Jeremiah used a simile to depict Israel's quasi-spiritual dilemma. He wrote: "A voice was heard in Ramah, a voice of lamentation and of woe. The voice of Rachel, *the quasi-spiritual mind,* weeping for her children and refusing to be comforted; for they are not." Remember when reading the Bible that all is a parallelism where the Word is translated into God's light – times and places, names and faces are of no consequence. Only the light of eternal truth shines through.

The fact that the soul is held captive by traditional worship does not, however, deprive man of redemption. Only his dark misconceptions are excluded. This is confirmed in an outpictured manner when the thief on the cross, *signifying the quasi-spiritual mind,* turns to Christ and repentantly pleads, "Lord, RE-MEMBER ME, *remember my spiritual heritage,* when you come in your Father's kingdom." To which Christ replies, "This day you shall be with me in Paradise," *in Spirit and in truth.* As for the murderer who was also crucified with Christ, he is comparable to the temporal mind and cannot be spiritually redeemed. ("The Word was crucified between two malefactors.") Nevertheless, without regard to the mind's progressive levels of comprehension, when linear thought gives way to parallel understanding the "whole man" is spiritualized. Quasi-spiritual thought is transposed, without error, and the unshakable truth that remains is received into the kingdom of heaven. ("Only those things that cannot be shaken will remain.") Referring to this flooding of the mind with Christ's redeeming light, Paul affirmed, "Now is our salvation nearer than we at first believed."

7

The Revelation Unfolds

"And God said, Let there be lights in the
firmament of the heaven to give light
upon the earth. And God made two
great lights; the greater light to rule the
day and the lesser light to rule the night.
He made the stars also."

GENESIS 1:14-16

The disclosures made in our previous discussions
were intended to provide a foundation for events
we are about to consider; events that begin with
Genesis and extend through the days of the prophets –
in all, a period of some four thousand years. Without
this preparatory knowledge, it would be fairly impossible to understand the symbolism relating to those
earlier times. While it would not be presumptuous to
assume the Creator had preplanned the direction of his
work, it is painfully clear that man had little knowledge
of God's intentions. Paul speaks of the limitations
encountered by the Bible's founding fathers when he
writes, "They saw in part and they prophesied in part."
But God's outpictured revelation came to an end with

Christ's death, his resurrection and his subsequent ascension. So, with that introductory age now past, we can now look beyond and interpret what, at the time, was seen only in part.

Since the authors of Scripture depended upon the history and understanding of their times to convey God's truth, their disclosures can be misleading. For instance, if taken literally, the reliability of the Creation story is questionable. Here, we are told that on the third day of Creation God said, "Let the earth bring forth after its own kind; grass and herb yielding seed and tree yielding fruit, whose seed is in itself." Then, on the fourth day he creates the sun, the moon and the stars, and sets them within the heavens "to give light upon the earth." In other words, the earth was in full bloom before the sun appeared in the heavens, before the atmosphere was formed, or before the clouds appeared to provide the earth with rain. Clearly, from a scientific viewpoint, something is amiss. The presentation is definitely out of sequence. But this can be explained. The Bible is not a scientific document; its truth is rooted in spiritual symbolism and should not be interpreted otherwise. ("Judge not according to the appearance, but judge right judgment.")

On the other hand, when Scripture's Word is converted from evolution to involution, we find the Creation story perfectly aligned with man's spiritual ascendancy. The fruits of the earth appear on the third day and relate to Adam's sensory body. This must precede the forming of the heavens, which appear on the fourth day and relate to the mind of Eve. Then, on the fifth day, the seas are formed, *the great "See" of knowledge,* and the waters thereof are teeming with life. The Creation story is an excellent example of the conflict that divides linear thought from parallel thought. ("No man puts new wine into old skins; for when the wine expands the skins are broken and both the skins and the wine are lost.")

In studying spiritual symbolism, we must always look beyond outer appearances. The scope of the Word's diversity is revealed in the Garden of Eden simile. As Genesis relates, "A river, *the light of Life*, went out of Eden to water the garden; and from thence it was parted and became four heads." We are thus informed that the light of Life, which began as a single river, divided and became four tributaries. The first tributary became the light of Life within the regenerative Principle, the second tributary became the light of Life within Creation's light-pattern, the third tributary became the light of Life within man, and the fourth tributary became the light of Life within the Word's instructional "signs and wonders." All was watered by the visible expressions God had accorded Christ.

However, when Adam and Eve ate of the Tree of Knowledge of good and evil and descended into temporal knowledge, the spiritual aspect of Eden's "river of Life" was lost. Consequently, the Bible expresses the number "four" in a negative manner. With Christ's resurrection, *the resurrection of the Word's reconciling work,* the outward flow of those four rivers, as they applied to man, was reversed and God's spiritual intentions for Adam were finally realized. All nations then began flowing into the "river of Life."

Because temporal man could relate only to his temporal world, Scripture depicts the number "four" as a symbol associated with deprivation and affliction. Consider the following:

- "His kingdom shall be broken and divided toward the *temporal* four winds."
- "Know of a certainty that your seed shall dwell in a *temporal* land that is not theirs; and they shall afflict them four hundred years."
- "The windows of heaven were opened and it rained forty days and forty nights upon the *temporal* earth."
- "Israel failed to believe God; and they wandered in the *temporal* wilderness of Sinai for forty years."
- "He shall send forth his angels and they shall gather his elect from the *temporal* four winds; from the one end of heaven to the other."

In a linear sense, each of these presentations appears as a historical event. But from a parallel viewpoint, all witness to a common principle. All speak of the affliction suffered by the spiritual aspect of God's light-pattern in Christ.

Moving forward to the symbolism represented by the three sons of Adam and Eve, we are told that Adam's firstborn son, Cain, was a tiller of the ground while his second-born son, Abel, was a keeper of flocks. Since "as a man sows, so shall he reap," their labors tell us that Cain harvested what grew in the soil, *the temporal*, while Abel harvested what grew above the soil, *the quasi-spiritual*. So we again see a line drawn between the temporal and quasi-spiritual minds. We are then informed that when Cain saw God had more respect for Abel's labors, he grew angry, and "in his anger, Cain arose and slew his brother." Cain's actions are significant because they reflect a phenomenon that remains with us to this day: The temporal mind, in its desire to prevail, has imposed a sentence of death upon the quasi-spiritual mind. The similitude of Cain claiming the life of his brother introduces us to an abstract state of reality, one that puts the quasi-spiritual mind to death. ("Why do you go about to kill me?") In that context, Jesus told the Jews, "Beware of the leaven of the scribes and Pharisees."

To ensure, that man should not lose his intended spiritual heritage, God gave Adam and Eve a third child, a son named Seth. The line of spiritual ascendancy thus passed through Abel to Seth and culminated with the birth of Jesus Christ. Through Seth's redeeming seed, he that suffered quasi-spiritual death – Abel – obtained life.

The importance of this simile is that it sets a precedent for future events. Paralleling the actions of Adam's three sons, the mind would now experience two additional states of reality. The first reality would be comparable to the mind of temporal Cain, the second reality would be comparable to the mind of quasi-spiritual Able, and the third reality would be comparable to the mind of spiritual Seth. The firstborn would follow sensory instincts and be earthy, the second-born would seek spiritual truth but fall prey to his earthy brother's jealousy, and the third-born would seek the Spirit of God and conform to his Spirit. ("In the third day he shall raise us up.")

Until we recognize that the world's theological community is influenced by the temporal mind, the events of the "Old Testament" cannot be understood. Make no mistake; by clinging to temporal understanding, both Judaism and Christianity have made the Word of God of non-effect. Paul described the Word's two readings as the "letter" of the Word and the "Spirit" of the Word. Noting that the Jews followed after the "letter" of the Word, he wrote, "I could wish myself cursed for Israel's sake." Also, John quotes Christ as saying, "I know the lies of those who say they are Jews and are not, but are the Synagogue of Satan." However, the Jews are not alone. "All have erred and fallen short of the glory of God."

Referring to man's conflicting thoughts, the Book of Revelation symbolically relates: "There was war in heaven. Michael and his angels, *the angels of light,* fought against Satan and his angels, *the angels of temporal darkness*, and Satan and his angels prevailed not. Neither was their place found anymore in heaven." When Cain slew his brother, Abel, the war in heaven began, and on the third day, when Christ was raised from the dead, the war in heaven ended. The events that transpired between those two occasions, in all some four thousand years, provided resolution for the mind's predicament. ("Choose this day whom you shall serve. As for me and my house, we shall serve the Lord.")

When we project Seth's lineage to the seventh from Adam, our attention is quickly drawn to Enoch, for we are told, "Enoch walked with God and was not; for God took him." Here, for the first time, man is recognized as a parallelism. When Enoch walked with God he discovered their COMMON-UNITY and THEY TWO BECAME ONE SPIRIT. ("In that day they shall not ask, Do you

know the Lord? For, they shall all be known of me.")
Thus, in Enoch, the windows of heaven were opened
and God's "true light" flooded in, covering the myriad
facets of glory he had made.

The Reflective Waters

"And God said, Let there be a
firmament in the midst of the waters,
and let it divide the waters under the
firmament from the waters above the
firmament. And God called the
firmament Heaven."

GENESIS 1:6-8

A wise man once conceded, "God is my mirror." It
seems appropriate to describe this deliberative
remark as "reflective" because when Adam was
formed in God's image and likeness, Man, in turn
became God's mirror. Yet, the one could not reflect upon
the other without an all-inclusive contrasting witness, a
spiritual "Way-shower." That interpretive Counselor, the
Christ that was embodied within Creation, subsequently
emerged as the Son of man. Through his analogies, the
potential for God and man to converse became a reality.
("I do only those things I see with the Father.")

While the symbolism in God's work is like "a house
of mirrors," no reflective component dominates earth's
setting more than its great expanse of water. Because

water has the inherent ability to reflect, it is akin to the reflective principle upon which all life is based. In that regard, Genesis tells us that in the beginning the entire earth was covered with water, that all was reflective, and darkness was upon the face of the deep. ("And the Spirit of God moved upon the face of the waters.") We thus recognize that all life on earth was to follow the mirroring pattern that appeared in the waters' primal mass at earth's inception. We then read that on the second day, "God divided the waters that were under the firmament, *knowledge of life relating to the below,* from the waters that were above the firmament, *knowledge of life relating to the above,* and God called the firmament, *the light of Life that emanated from the midst of these two witnesses,* Heaven." Once we understand the dividing of the waters signifies the Creating of two reflective mirrors, our concept of "Heaven" is no longer seen as far off.

The dividing of the waters wherein the principle of "heaven" acquires manifestation appears on the third day, when God says, "Let the waters under the heaven, *knowledge relating to the below,* be gathered together unto one place and let the dry land appear." The "dry land" then emerges from the midst of the waters as an earthy replica of heaven. Therein, heaven and earth begin witnessing to each other as mutually reflective entities. In relationship to man, the waters under the firmament – which signified visible Creation – served as a conjunctive mirror through which man could communicate with God. As Genesis explains, "The Spirit of God moved upon the face of the waters." Or, as expressed in Eden's simile, "The Lord walked in the midst of the garden."

The Jewish tradition refers to this reflective attribute by using the axiom, "As above, so below." The Christian tradition affirms the same through the Lord's Prayer saying, "Thy kingdom come, thy will be done on earth as it is in heaven." When the prophet discovered that God's Spirit appeared within temporal manifestation, he wrote, "Holy, holy, holy is the Lord of hosts. Heaven and earth are full of his glory."

With the outpicturing of heaven into earth, *the above into the below,* the invisible became visible. Then, by passing Creation's visible setting through Adam's sensory faculties, the visible again became invisible. Therein, Eve – as an extension of Adam's sensory faculties – acquired the invisible aspect of the Creator's nature and conscious thought became the invisible equivalent of the above being mirrored into the below. The faculties of Eve's mind represented the waters above the firmament and the faculties of Adam's body represented the waters under the firmament – the "dry land." Mind and body were thus filled with heaven's glory.

Since Creation was designed to mirror the Creator's diverse attributes, heaven can be defined as "any place where God's Self-knowledge resides." So, when we read that God entered into his rest on the seventh day, it means that upon completing his work, he rested in the Self-knowledge his work provided. In keeping with this explanation, whenever the mind's "true light" relates to God's knowledge of himself, it enters into the "Paradise" of God's eternal "rest." ("And this is life eternal: to know God.")

Most religious doctrines teach that when the temporal body dies, *when it forfeits its temporal view of life*, it goes to heaven, but they do not teach that the temporal mind cannot enter heaven before knowing God. The one is not without the other. Christ affirmed this truth when he said, "No man has ascended into heaven, except he that came down from heaven; even the Son of man, *the Spirit of truth*, which is in heaven." Having defined heaven as anyplace where God's knowledge of himself resides, we have only to recognize the mind's temporal and spiritual configurations to know the kingdom of heaven exists as a constant. It has nothing in common with time or place. ("The kingdom of God comes not with observation.") Rather, it is the unifying of the mind's "two witnesses" and their ascent into that light presently expressed as Life's Ultimate Reality.

When we transpose the forming of God's heaven into man, the mind's temporal and quasi-spiritual aspects are equivalent to the darkness that was upon the face of the deep. The firmament of "heaven" is equivalent to the light that gives Life to the mind's various levels of comprehension. The waters gathered together under heaven relate to the mind's temporal understanding of life – the "dry land." The waters gathered together above the heaven relate to the mind's spiritual understanding of life. Since life's temporal and quasi-spiritual levels of comprehension cannot see heaven until their knowledge is translated into spiritual symbolism, we find the prophet, John the Baptist, exiting from the wilderness, *as a symbol of quasi-spiritual worship*, as the forerunner of Christ. He then assumes the role of one preaching the coming "day of the Lord." He baptizes those who believe his word in the Jordan's quasi-spiritual waters, and declares, "He that comes after me, *the spiritual*, is preferred before me, *the quasi-spiritual*, because he was before me. He must increase and I must decrease." Comparing John's baptism with the one Christ would perform in Spirit and in truth, Christ said: "John baptized with *temporal* water but I baptize with *spiritual* fire and with the Holy Ghost. He that is least in the kingdom of heaven is greater than John." That is, he that is spiritual is greater than he that is quasi-spiritual.

This brings us to Paul's realization that all of the early fathers were baptized under the cloud and in the sea. That is, their minds remained "clouded" because they failed to "see" and personalize the "signs and wonders" of God's work within themselves. Consequently, they continued living in an abstract state of existence. Nonetheless, as herein explained, the cloud was eventually taken up, "and the glory of the Lord appeared within the cloud," *within that symbolism that confirmed the glory of God in man.* ("I am your exceeding great reward.")

Although Scripture specifically associates the cloud with Israel's quasi-spiritual worship, that same cloud appears wherever traditional worship is practiced. Similes of God's presence within the cloud are identified in the following:

- "The glory of the Lord appeared in the cloud – *appeared in his veiled symbolism.*"
- "He has covered heaven with his cloud – *with his veiled symbolism.*"
- "His truth reaches to the clouds – *to his veiled symbolism.*"
- "He makes the cloud his chariot – *makes veiled symbolism his chariot.*"

- "Behold, he comes with clouds; and every eye shall see him – *he comes with veiled symbolism.*"
- "They shall see the Son of man coming on the clouds of heaven – *on heaven's veiled symbolism* – with power and great glory."

When the book of Job relates, "And now men see not the bright light that is in the cloud, except the wind, *the Spirit of truth,* passes and cleanses them"; it confirms that God's light remains hidden until the mind understands the Word's symbolic translation, *its second reading,* which is Christ's "second coming." ("To those who look for him, he shall appear a second time; *without temporal or quasi-spiritual error,* unto life eternal.")

Since spiritual and quasi-spiritual symbolism are reflective parallelisms, we see the waters gathered together in the below, *appearing in nature as rivers and oceans,* reflecting the "true light" within the cloud that is mirrored from above. Therein, the below portrays the Spirit of God moving upon the face of the waters, *moving upon the face of mankind's quasi-spiritual thought.* ("He that rests in the Lord shall abide under the shadow of his wings.") Man's quasi-spiritual witness is thus recognized as a veiled extension of Creation's inherent truth.

Pursuant to this reflective parallelism, we see the clouds veiling the Sun, obscuring the "true light" that gives life to the earth, and we see the windows of heaven, *the clouds of heaven,* opened, sending their rain upon the just and the unjust. And where there is rain there is also thunder, and when he speaks, "He thunders marvelously." And where there is thunder there is also lightning, and with those flashes of light he enlightens his heaven from east to west. Testifying to the reflective truths conveyed in God's work, the psalmist writes: "The heavens declare the glory of God; and the firmament shows forth his handiwork. He speaks in the day and gives knowledge to the night. There is no speech or language where their voice is not heard."

In discussing the reflective ability of water, we inevitably come to the great deluge that marked the days of Noah and his family. Remembering that biblical history portrays man's various stages of development, the opening of the "windows of heaven," and the chaotic downpour that enveloped the earth for forty days and forty nights, signaled an end to the mind's temporal reign and the beginning of its quasi-spiritual reign. When the book of Daniel discloses, "The end shall be in a flood," he refers to the flooding of the mind with a new form of knowledge. Jesus used the great deluge as a metaphor for the coming demise of errors that burdened quasi-spiritual thought when he related, "As it was in the days of Noah when the flood came and took them all away, so shall it be in the days of the Son of man." Using that historic event as a simile, the Spirit of God is again seen moving upon the face of the waters – this time with Noah and his family and the two of every kind that entered into the Ark. Subsequent to that deluge, man would acquire a higher level of cognizance – and a new heaven and a new earth would be formed.

The significance of that inundating event is that it marked a step forward in mankind's spiritual comprehension. Keep in mind, however, that historical events only reflect what man brings into the world. Events never change the man; it is the man who changes events. So, the continuous whole remained.

The Three Patriarchs

"And God said, Let there be lights in the firmament of the heaven to divide the day from the night; and let them be for signs, and for seasons, and for days, and for years. And let them be for lights in the firmament of the heaven to give light upon the earth: and it was so."

GENESIS 1:14-15

After the waters of the great deluge had subsided, man was introduced to a quasi-spiritual world. Nevertheless, being subject to the principle of the continuous whole, the false gods of temporal Reason continued to rule the earth. Since the pattern of things pertaining to the above had yet to be recognized, true spiritual understanding was still withheld. One of man's "reasonable" attempts to communicate with the above was to build a city having a tower that reached all the way to heaven (The Tower of Babel). Unaware that the road to spiritual understanding was not built with bricks and mortar, their labors came to nothing. Their language was confounded and the city was never completed. ("Except the Lord build the house, they labor in vain that build it.") Thereafter, the builders were scattered throughout the earth.

ABRAHAM

Without detailing the many spiritual failures of mankind, an effort of a much higher calling was finally initiated. This new effort began when God called to Abraham, saying, "Depart from your country, your kindred and your father's house, and go to a land that I will show you (The Promised Land) and I will make of you a great nation." However, God's covenant with Abraham was conditional. The covenant hinged upon the Patriarch leaving his homeland, his friends and his family. In other words, being of a temporal mind he had to "sacrifice" his temporal heritage. This was the pattern set forth from the beginning, when God's light emerged from the dark void. This was the "sure foundation" on which the kingdom of God would be built. This prerequisite is set forth in the following instruction:

- "He that seeks his life must lose it; and he that will lose his life for my sake and the kingdom of God, shall find it unto life eternal."
- "He that loves father or mother more than me is not worthy of me; and he that loves son or daughter more than me is not worthy of me."
- "He that goes forth in sorrow, bearing precious seed, shall doubtless come again with rejoicing, bringing his sheaves with him."

○ "It is expedient for you that I go away; for if I go not away the Spirit of truth, *the light of Life which is revealed in the Word's second reading,* will not come."

○ "They could not enter into his rest because of unbelief."

Few things contribute more to man's spiritual progress than understanding the necessity for "voiding temporal knowledge." The day that Abraham departed from his native land, he joined forces with The Eternal. As Christ told the Jews, "Abraham rejoiced to see my day; and he saw it and was glad." Abraham responded to God's calling in a positive way. He departed with his entourage and journeyed into the land of Canaan. Having passed beyond its borders, the Lord again appeared to him, saying, "Unto your seed will I give this land."

But the time for Abraham receiving his promised inheritance had not yet come. The land was not yet converted and there was famine in Canaan. So, after building two altars to the Lord, *symbolizing the land's approaching passover from temporal to quasi-spiritual understanding,* Abraham resumed his journey and traveled southward into Egypt, *signifying the mind's continuing sojourn in a temporal state.*

To understand Egypt's role in God's plan, we again return to the mind's most powerful faculty: Reason. Historically, Egypt was known as "the dark land" and Pharaoh was called "the god of the earth." So, as an analogy, Pharaoh represented the faculty of Reason and Egypt represented the temporal darkness over which he reigned. Upon entering Egypt, Abraham was forced to conceal his true relationship with his wife, Sarah, *the quasi-spiritual mind,* and this he did by presenting her to Pharaoh and the princes of Egypt as his sister. Because of Sarah's beauty, Abraham was favored, and by taking advantage of his status in Egypt, he became very wealthy. But Pharaoh eventually discovered his secret: that God had favored Abraham by making Sarah his wife. Fearing the wrath of Abraham's God, Pharaoh asked the Patriarch to leave his land and Abraham complied. Taking the wealth he had acquired in Egypt, Abraham journeyed back to Canaan; to the land God had promised to him and his seed for an inheritance.

It is important to note that upon departing from Egypt, Abraham took the wealth and influences of Egypt's temporal state with him. We thus see the quasi-spiritual mind directly influenced by the temporal mind. Attesting to that influence, Sarah brought her Egyptian servant, Hagar, to the land of Canaan. Later, Hagar became the mother of Ishmael, Abraham's first-born son. Many years later, when she was beyond her childbearing years, Sarah also conceived – giving Abraham a second son, Isaac. As was foretold to Abraham, "In Isaac, shall your seed be called."

Although by tradition the firstborn son, *the temporal mind,* always received the father's blessing, God nullified that practice and chose Isaac, Abraham's second-born son, the quasi-spiritual mind. This was in keeping with the path of mankind's progressive ascendancy, *his passing from temporal to quasi-spiritual reality.* We thus see the mind's first and second realities characterized in Ishmael and Isaac. These two forms of thought would dominate the psyche until the days of the prophets, at which time the mind would evolve into a third reality; namely the spiritual "Son of man."

When God initially called to Abraham and instructed him to depart from his native land, his entourage included his brother's son, Lot, *Lot portraying the mind's temporal nature.* And when Abraham journeyed from Canaan into Egypt, Lot remained with him. When Abraham departed from Egypt with his accumulated wealth, Lot likewise departed with great substance. When Abraham and Lot returned to Canaan their combined substance and cattle were far more than the land could bear. To resolve the problem, Abraham said to Lot: "Choose for yourself the land wherein you and your herdsman will dwell. If you go to the left, then I will go to the right." Not settling for less than what appeared best, Lot chose the fertile plain of Jordan and journeyed to the east, and Abraham remained in Canaan.

Among the cities of Jordan's lower plain, *the temporal plain of mind and body,* lay Sodom and Gomorrah. Morally, the people that dwelt in these two cities were exceedingly evil; so evil that God foresaw their demise. Knowing that Lot resided in Sodom, Abraham persuaded God to send emissaries to warn Lot and his family of the city's impending doom. To escape an untimely end, Lot and his family fled the city – being forewarned by the emissaries not to look back. However, when fire and brimstone rained down upon the twin cities, Lot's wife looked back. As a result she was turned into a pillar of salt.

Christ brought this event into spiritual perspective by using the following parallelism:

"As it was in the days of Lot, so shall it be in the days of the Son of man, *in the days of the mind's departure from temporal understanding.*

They did eat, they drank, they bought, they sold, they planted and they built; but the same day that Lot departed from Sodom it rained fire and brimstone from heaven and destroyed them all.

So shall it be in the days when the Son of man is revealed."

You will find the "pattern" of Abraham's walk with God detailed in the book of Genesis. His deeds witness to the Lord's abiding presence. He dwelt in the land that God had promised to him and to his seed for an inheritance and there he purchased a burial place. And when the days of Abraham and Sarah were fulfilled, they were gathered unto the Father's eternal Spirit.

ISAAC

While it is important to recognize that all generations share in life's continuous whole, we should not forget that each individual is viewed as "a work in progress." We must therefore evolve through the various stages of reality experienced by our predecessors before we can achieve true spirituality. Following Christ's lead, we must each finish the work God has given us to do. This personal re-knowing of the mind's "true light" is again mirrored in the story of Isaac.

Since the lives and times of the three Patriarchs centered on translating externalized manifestation into quasi-spiritual thought, it followed that what they recognized they took literally. Therefore, when Abraham was asked to sacrifice his second-born son, Isaac, as an offering to God, cleansed by fire, *signifying the need to sacrifice the literal aspect of quasi-spiritual thought to gain spiritual truth,* he immediately built a sacrificial altar on which to offer his son. There is no doubt that Abraham misread God's intentions. The psalmist assures us of this when he writes: "Sacrifice and offering God did not desire. Burnt offerings and sin offerings he did not require." Obviously, Abraham could not distinguish between temporal and spiritual understanding. Although the Spirit of God led the Patriarch, he had yet to seek and to save that which remained lost within himself.

Therefore, after Abraham had built his sacrificial altar and was about to begin his ritualistic offering of Isaac, the angel of the Lord appeared and showed him "a lamb caught in the thicket," *a symbol of the "true light" that was entangled in the mind's temporal perceptions; a lamb Abraham was to sacrifice instead of Isaac.* Christianity recognizes this "lamb of God" as a Christ type, but until this symbol of personal sacrifice is spiritually interpreted it has no impact. As previously explained, the Word has two readings. The lamb caught in the thicket represents the quasi-spiritual mind becoming entangled in temporal misconceptions. THIS ENTANGLED WORD MUST BE SACRIFICED! However, such a feat would not be accomplished on a spiritual plane until some 1,260 years later; until the fulfilling of the days of God's external "signs and wonders." At that time, the Spirit of

Life from God would enter into those redemptive similes and the externalized "Arm of the Lord" would be internalized as "the Son of man"; an event referred to in Scripture as "The First Resurrection."

Since God had chosen the three Patriarchs to serve as his anointed revelators, they dutifully conformed to Creation's law that every seed should bring forth after its own kind. They therefore refused to take wives, *temporal thought,* from among the Gentiles. So when Isaac became old enough to marry he sought a woman of his own lineage, one that was related to his father's house. He commissioned his servant to return to the land wherein Abraham was called. There, he was to seek a daughter from the family of Abraham's sister-in-law to become Isaac's wife. Directed by the Lord, the servant chose Rebekah, and she returned with Isaac's servant to the land of Canaan. There, in the land God had promised to Abraham, Isaac and Rebekah were married.

Rebekah eventually gave birth to twin sons: Esau, the firstborn, and Jacob, the second-born. Symbolically, the birth of these two mirrored the division between the temporal and quasi-spiritual minds; so upon coming into the world, Jacob's hand, *the mind's quasi-spiritual knowledge,* was upon Esau's heel, *the mind that held fast to temporal understanding.*

When the boys grew older Esau became a hunter and a man of the field, while Jacob became a shepherd and dwelt in tents – a relationship comparable to that of Cain and Abel. One day when Esau came in from the fields feeling exceedingly tired and hungry, Jacob persuaded him to exchange his birthright, *the right of the firstborn to receive the father's blessing,* for some food, and Esau agreed. That day, Jacob manipulated

Esau and robbed him of his birthright. Again, when Isaac was old and could not see, Jacob tricked his father into bestowing the promises of God upon him. He thus obtained the covenant God had made with Abraham and Isaac. As the victim of Jacob's scheming ways, Esau was cheated out of his birthright for a second time, and the promises made to Abraham and his seed passed to the second-born son. The quasi-spiritual deception that was signaled at the birth of Rebekah's twin sons was thus fulfilled.

Isaac and Rebekah lived out their days in the land of Canaan. An account of their lives can be found in the book of Genesis. They were buried beside Abraham and Sarah in the field that Abraham had purchased for a burial place. In keeping with the covenant God had made with Abraham, they were gathered unto their Father's eternal Spirit.

JACOB

After Jacob had twice robbed Esau – first of his temporal birthright, then of his quasi-spiritual inheritance in God – hatred mounted between Isaac's two sons. Fearing that Esau would kill his brother, Rebekah advised Jacob to flee from Canaan and return to the house of her brother, Laban. Jacob hastily agreed. What Jacob had failed to understand was that in obtaining his father's blessing and the promises made to Abraham, personal sacrifice was required. ("He that seeks his life must lose it.") Nevertheless, fearing Esau would slay him, Jacob departed from Canaan and turned eastward toward the land of Laban.

As he journeyed into the evening and the sun went down, Jacob stopped and made camp for the night. He took stones and made a pillow for his head, then fell asleep. As he slept he dreamed of a ladder, *God's instructional "signs and wonders,"* set upon the earth, whose top reached up to heaven, and he saw the angels of God, *heaven's revelatory truths,* ascending and descending upon its steps. Above the ladder God appeared, and from this most high place the Lord bestowed the blessings of Abraham and Isaac upon him. When Jacob arose from his sleep he was frightened, and he said: "Surely God is in this place; and I knew it not. This is none other than the house of God and the gate to heaven." This symbolic characterization of the Word's two readings is referred to when Jesus tells his disciples, "Hereafter, you shall see heaven opened and the angels of God ascending and descending upon the Son of man."

After Jacob had arrived at the house of Laban and was made welcome, he began serving his uncle as the keeper of his flocks. Laban had two daughters: Leah, the firstborn, *the temporal,* and Rachel, the second-born, *the quasi-spiritual.* Because of her beauty, Jacob fell in love with Rachel. He asked Laban for her hand in marriage and it was agreed that Jacob should serve Laban for seven years and Rachel would then be his. But when the seven years were fulfilled, Laban tricked Jacob into marrying Leah – his temporal-minded daughter. Aware of Jacob's anger, Laban promised that if he would serve another seven years he could also have Rachel. Jacob agreed. Finally, after serving Laban for fourteen years, he married Rachel. Jacob's acquisition of two wives, *the first of a temporal nature, the second of a quasi-spiritual nature,* reflects his divided state of mind and his mistreatment of Esau and Isaac. But Jacob had yet to learn his lesson. The thoughts of his heart would continually afflict him, bringing much sorrow to his days.

Jacob stayed with Laban for many years, during which time he sired six sons and one daughter by Leah, and two sons by Zilpah, Leah's handmaid. He also had one son, Joseph, by Rachel, and two sons by Bilhah, Rachel's handmaid. In all, there were eleven sons: seven by the married wives, four by their handmaids. The size of Laban's flocks also grew, and Jacob realized it was time for him to return to Canaan.

He therefore approached his father-in-law with the suggestion that he receive a portion of Laban's cattle as payment for his years of service. Laban agreed. He determined, they would go through the cattle and remove all the speckled and spotted and brown from the flock, and these would become Jacob's cattle. The unspotted would belong to Laban. A division was thus made between the two flocks, and Jacob instructed his sons to take the spotted and brown cattle a three days' journey into the country. Jacob remained with Laban and cared for his remaining flock. However, wanting more in return for his labors, he devised a method of making Laban's newborn cattle appear speckled and spotted. He fouled the water and forced the strongest animals to drink the fouled water. Consequently, blemishes appeared in their coats and the newborn cattle became Jacob's.

When Jacob saw Laban was growing increasingly angry over the diminishing size of his flock, he assembled his household and all of their goods and stole away in secret. Three days after his departure, Laban discovered Jacob's deception and pursued him toward Canaan. After confronting his son-in-law, however, the two were reconciled and each went his own way.

As Jacob continued his journey back to Canaan, he again stopped for the night. When darkness fell, a man approached him, and the two wrestled with each other throughout the night. As dawn arrived the man said, "Let me go!" But Jacob replied, "I will not let you go until you bless me." And he that wrestled with Jacob blessed him, saying, "You shall no more be called Jacob, but Israel, *by interpretation, a prince of God*, for you have power with God and have prevailed with men." Thereafter, the man departed and Jacob returned to Canaan where he was reunited with Esau.

In later years Rachel again conceived and gave birth to a second son, Benjamin, *the second wife, who characterized the quasi-spiritual mind, gave birth to a second son, one who characterized the spiritual mind.* Rachel, *the quasi-spiritual mind,* died giving birth to Benjamin, *her spiritual son,* and was buried in Bethlehem, *by interpretation, the house of bread,* in Canaan. In all, twelve sons were born to Jacob, and the lineage of those twelve gave birth to the nation of Israel.

As for Jacob, famine in the land of Canaan would one day force him to return to Egypt, where he would live out his days. At length, he would confess to Pharaoh, "My days have been few and full of evil," and he would go his way blessing Pharaoh. Jacob died in the land of Egypt and his son Joseph carried his body back to Canaan for burial.

There, the three Patriarchs rested together and they were gathered unto their Father's eternal Spirit.

10

Joseph and His Brethren

"And Joseph consoled his brothers,
saying: You thought evil against me but
God turned it into good. Had I not been
sold into Egypt I could not have saved
the lives of my brethren from the famine
that now plagues the earth."

GENESIS 50:20

As events clearly indicate, the quasi-spiritual mantle of the three Patriarchs came to rest on the shoulders of Joseph, the firstborn son of Rachel, Jacob's second wife. And Jacob loved Rachel's son above the others, which created increasing jealousy and hatred amongst the other brothers.

In keeping with this attachment, when Joseph was seventeen years of age Jacob made him "a coat of many colors," *a coat of many symbols*, which foretold who would inherit the Patriarch's quasi-spiritual mantle. The mystery behind the coat is revealed by its description, for the coat's colorful pieces mirrored the shades of spiritual symbolism Joseph was chosen to personify. But seeing their father's favoritism, the brothers grew increasingly resentful.

Their hatred for Joseph reached its height when they were told of his two dreams. In the first dream, the sons of Jacob were together in the fields binding sheaves when suddenly Joseph's sheave stood upright and his brothers' sheaves bowed before it, *the bowing of the mind's lower reality to its higher reality.* In the second dream, Joseph saw the sun and the moon and eleven stars bowing before him. This second dream relates to his inheriting the "true light" that resides within the Word's quasi-spiritual authority, a light to which all of the Sons of God witness. The two dreams signified that the Word of the Lord now rested upon Joseph, and that heaven and earth would be his "two witnesses." Upon hearing his two dreams, Joseph's brothers were consumed with rage.

Overwhelmed by their passion, they plotted to kill Joseph. But Judah interceded, suggesting they sell their brother to a caravan of traders headed for Egypt. They all agreed. Stripping Joseph of his colorful coat, they smeared goat's blood over its pieces. Then, upon returning to their father's house, they presented Jacob with the bloodstained coat and told him Joseph had been killed and eaten by a great beast. Their father believed them. Thus, in the person of Joseph, the Word of the Lord descended into Egypt's dark land to dwell in the house of Pharaoh, the god-man of all the earth.

When the traders arrived in Egypt, they sold Joseph as a slave to Potiphar, a captain of Pharaoh's guard. But when Potiphar saw that the Lord was with Joseph and that all he did prospered, he made Joseph ruler over all of his wealth. "And the Lord blessed Potiphar's house for Joseph's sake."

As events unfolded, Pharaoh dreamed two dark similitudes that troubled him. He called in his magicians and wise men to interpret the dreams, but none could explain their meaning. His butler, having discovered by a previous experience that Joseph could interpret dreams, suggested that Pharaoh seek his counsel. Appearing before Egypt's king, Joseph was asked if he could explain the dreams. He replied, "It is not in me to interpret dreams; but God will give you the answer." So Pharaoh disclosed the nature of the dreams that troubled him.

He explained, "In my dream I stood by a river and seven well-favored cattle – *the quasi-spiritual mind* – came up from the water and grazed in the meadow. After that, seven ill-favored cattle – *the temporal mind* – came up and devoured the first." In the second dream, he related, "I saw seven ears of corn, full and good, on one stalk. Then seven others, withered and thin, came up and devoured the good ears." Interpreting the dreams, Joseph said: "The two dreams are one. God is showing Pharaoh what he is about to do in Egypt. The seven good ears of corn – *God's quasi-spiritual 'signs and wonders' in Israel* – are seven years of plenty, and the seven withered ears of corn – *the mind's temporal knowledge in Egypt* – are seven years of famine." The famine of the later years, when the entire land is made desolate, shall feed on the plenty of the former years. By harvesting the years of plenty, provision is made, *through translation*, for the spiritual years that follow. Pharaoh's dream thus represented a twofold parallelism. In both presentations, the stronger entity – *the quasi-spiritual "signs and wonders" that were devoured by the temporal mind* – would, in the time of famine, sustain the temporal mind. The temporal mind would therefore survive at the expense of God's instructive "signs and wonders." As Christ explained, "Behold, there are last which shall be first, and there are first which shall be last."

Joseph further advised Pharaoh: "Seek out a man, *a Way-shower,* discreet and wise, and set him over the land of Egypt. Have him lay in store the fifth part of the harvest during the seven years of plenty. This, save against the seven years of famine that shall follow." Pharaoh listened to Joseph's counsel and, because God had revealed Egypt's future to him, Pharaoh made Joseph ruler over all the land, *symbolically, the quasi-spiritual mind was to rule over the temporal, just as the spiritual mind would eventually rule over the quasi-spiritual.* In Egypt, Joseph was second only to Pharaoh – *the quasi-spiritual was still ruled by temporal Reason.* Joseph was thirty years old when he became Egypt's overseer – *when the mind's forthcoming desolation was revealed through him.*

To further show his gratitude, Pharaoh provided Joseph with a wife – the daughter of an Egyptian priest. By her, Joseph had two sons: Manasseh, the firstborn, and Ephraim, the second-born. Joseph ruled in the land, gathering one-fifth of the harvest to set in store against the seven years of famine yet to come. When the famine God had foretold came upon Egypt, Joseph opened the storehouses of plenty, *the Word's "bread of Life,"* and sold its substance to all who came before him.

Meanwhile, the children of Israel in Canaan were also suffering from famine. Therefore, upon hearing that food was available in Egypt, Jacob sent ten of his sons to purchase their needs. But he kept Benjamin, *the spiritual*, with him; for he said, "If I lose Benjamin I shall surely die."

When the sons of Jacob arrived in Egypt and appeared before Joseph with their requests for food, they failed to recognize their brother; they thought Joseph was dead. But Joseph knew his brothers. Wishing to conceal his identity, he allowed the ten to speak with him – but only through a translator. Upon questioning their intentions, they informed him they were twelve sons of one man, but one son was dead and the other was at home with his father. Joseph then accused the ten of being spies. They tried to assure him they were not. To test their honesty, he placed Simeon in prison and told the remaining nine to return to Canaan and bring their brother Benjamin to him. "If you refuse you shall never see my face again," he warned. The nine reluctantly complied and returned to Canaan. Convincing Jacob that Benjamin would be safe with them, the brothers returned to Egypt for a second time. Joseph and Benjamin, the two sons of Rachel, *the quasi-spiritual and the spiritual*, were thus united.

In keeping with the dream of Joseph's youth, the eleven sons of Jacob bowed before him. Joseph forgave his brethren for having sold him to traders, and the reconciliation of the twelve was complete. Joseph then made provision to bring Israel and all of his children into Egypt, that their lives might be spared. This was a prelude to the fulfillment of the prophecy in which God told Abraham: "Be assured that your seed shall be a stranger in a land that is not theirs, and they shall afflict them four hundred years. And that nation whom they shall serve, I will judge; and afterward I will bring them out with great substance." So Israel left the land God had promised to Abraham and his seed, and settled in Goshen of Egypt.

As the famine in Egypt worsened, the inhabitants of the land came to buy food from Joseph and he took their money. And when their money was gone he took their cattle. And when their cattle were gone he took their land. Eventually, THERE WAS NOTHING IN EGYPT THAT DID NOT BELONG TO PHARAOH. When the famine finally subsided, Joseph provided seed for replanting throughout Egypt and told the people, "From henceforth, four parts of the harvest shall be yours; but the fifth part shall belong to Pharaoh." And so it was.

When Joseph saw that his father had grown old and was about to die, he brought his two sons, Manasseh and Ephraim, before Jacob to receive his blessing. He stood Manasseh, his firstborn, at Jacob's right hand, and Ephraim, his second-born, at Jacob's left hand. But when Israel stretched forth his hands to bless the boys he crossed his arms, placing his right hand upon Ephraim and his left hand upon Manasseh. Knowing his father's eyes were failing, Joseph thought he had made a mistake and tried to redirect Jacob's hands. But Israel said, "Not so! The second-born shall be greater than the firstborn." And the boys were blessed accordingly. The mantle of quasi-spiritual authority was thus passed from Joseph to his second-born son, Ephraim. However, since the mother of Manasseh and Ephraim was Egyptian, in the later days Ephraim would bow to Judah and be subject to the lawgiver – to the principles embodied in the law of Moses.

After blessing the sons of Joseph, Israel assembled his twelve sons that they, too, might receive his blessing. He blessed each of the twelve, paralleling the Word of the Lord to what he saw of his sons within himself. Placing all within the framework of the quasi-spiritual mind, he perceived God's Word in Joseph as "a fruitful bough whose branches extended to the well of life." He also saw God's light in Joseph as adversarial; a Spirit despised and rejected of men. Nevertheless, he foresaw the quasi-spiritual mind within Joseph becoming "the cornerstone of Israel," a sure foundation upon which God would build and judge all nations.

Israel likened the Word of the Lord in Judah to an avenging law, "as a lion that arose and devoured its prey." And of this governing law he said: "He crouched, he stooped as a lion; and who shall raise him up? The scepter shall not depart from Judah until Shiloh comes, *until the Word's 'true light' appears,* and unto Shiloh shall be the gathering of the people." Understand that Israel's blessings were not confined to his sons alone, but applied to all people; for Israel's pattern of light was equal to the Word of the Lord, the "true light" that is found in all.

As foretold, the children of Israel remained in Egypt four hundred years. They were taken into captivity and perished in a land that was not theirs. After the days of their captivity were fulfilled, Egypt was spoiled. With a mighty hand and with great substance, God brought them to Sinai. Their exodus from Egypt would be commemorated forever, for it marked "the feast of Passover" wherein God's Word would awaken man and lead him to his eternal heritage.

"Arise, walk through the land in the length of it and the breadth of it; for I will give it to you and your seed forever."

Moses and the Exodus

"And the daughter of Pharaoh called the
Hebrew child Moses: because she said,
I drew him out of the waters."

EXODUS 2:10

The history of Israel's captivity in Egypt is a
mirroring of humanity's ongoing spiritual deprivation. Outpictured, it is a period when the
descendants of Abraham were void of all spiritual
communication with their God. Essentially, they were
reduced to a nation of "believers," a people of "hope," a
people WAITING FOR A DELIVERER TO COME AND
SAVE THEM. So Israel waited for a sign from God, a
sign that their departure from Egypt was imminent;
and they waited four hundred years!

While in Egypt, the children of Israel grew in number
from a few family members into a great multitude; so
much that the Egyptians began to fear them. To
prevent Israel's supremacy, Pharaoh placed the
Hebrews in bondage and made their lives bitter. When
the children of Israel continued to multiply, Pharaoh
decreed that all newborn Hebrew male children should

be drowned in the rivers of Egypt, and it was done according to Pharaoh's word. However, there was an exception: a son born into the family of Levi, who was saved by his mother. She built an ark of bulrushes and daubed it with slime and pitch to make it watertight. She then placed her newborn son within the ark and set him adrift upon the river. And the Spirit of God within the child moved upon the face of the waters.

To see where the river would bear the ark, she sent her daughter to hide amongst the reeds and watch. Meanwhile, the daughter of Pharaoh came down to the river to wash, and when she saw the ark she called to her maidens to bring the basket to her. When she opened the ark and found the Hebrew child within, she decided to keep it for herself. She named the child "Moses." Pharaoh's daughter then brought the child into her father's house and raised him. Moses was thus educated in the ways of Egypt's wise men and priests.

It was not until he became a man that Moses became aware of his Hebrew lineage and discovered the truth that he was born to a Levite family. Moses went out and saw how the Egyptians burdened his brethren, and it grieved him. Then, by chance, Moses came upon an Egyptian guard beating one of the Hebrews. Unable to control his wrath, he slew the guard and buried him in the sand. Word circulated among the people of what Moses had done and he was afraid it would be told to Pharaoh. Fearing for his life, he departed from Egypt and fled across the wilderness to the land of Midian.

In Midian, Moses came upon a well and sat beside it to rest. While refreshing himself, the seven daughters of Jethro – a descendent of Ishmael and a priest of Midian – came to water their father's flock. While the girls were fulfilling their task, other shepherds came and drove them away. Seeing their distress, Moses came to their aid. He stood up to the intruders and they scattered, and Jethro's daughters returned. Afterward, at Jethro's request, the daughters brought Moses to their father's house. There he remained and served as a shepherd of Midian. In time, Jethro gave his firstborn daughter, Zipporah, to Moses for a wife, and he continued serving his father-in-law as a shepherd, watching over his flock.

One day Moses led Jethro's herd to the foot of Sinai, a mount that bordered on the desert. There, the angel of the Lord appeared to him, radiating as a flame of fire from the midst of a bush. Curious to see how the bush could burn without being consumed, *comparable to God's quasi-spiritual "signs and wonders" providing the mind with spiritual light without being understood,* Moses turned to view this wonder more closely. When God saw Moses approaching, he said: "Moses, come no closer. Take the shoes from your feet, for the ground on which you stand, *the sign 'I' of your knowledge,* is holy ground." Thus, through the angel of the Lord, *through a simile that mirrored the mind's quasi-spiritual Word of knowledge – Moses came face-to-face with God,* the light of Life that dwelt in the midst of Creation and was later personified as Christ.

The Word of the Lord continued speaking to Moses from the midst of the fire, saying, "I am the God of Abraham, the God of Isaac, and the God of Jacob." And Moses covered his face, for he was afraid to look upon God. Then the voice said: "I have heard the cry of my people in Egypt. I have seen their bondage and how the Egyptians afflict them. Come, therefore, and I will send you to bring Israel out of Egypt; and they shall serve me in Sinai" – in sign "I."

Overwhelmed by the magnitude of his calling, Moses asked God to excuse him from the task. But he refused. Moses then asked, "What shall I say to the children of Israel when they ask who sent me?" And the Lord replied: "You shall say I AM has sent you. I AM that I AM." Moses reluctantly complied. Taking his wife and his sons with him, he returned to Egypt and to his Hebrew brethren who remained in bondage.

When God identified himself to Moses as, "I AM that I AM," he provided mankind with a three-dimensional insight into the Word's all-inclusive character. These three insights are as follows:

- He confirmed that the "I AM," *the light within Creation,* was the image and likeness of the "I AM," *the light within its Creator.*
- He confirmed that the "I AM," *the light within man,* was the image and likeness of the "I AM," *the light within Creation.*
- He confirmed that the "I AM," *the light in the Word's outpictured revelation,* God's *"signs and wonders,"* was the image and likeness of the "I AM," *the light within man and Creation.*

Christ emphasized his role in the above when he told the multitude, "No man knows the Son, *the true light,* except the Father, *the Life within the light,* and no man knows the Father except the Son and he to whom the Son, *the light within the Life,* reveals him." His analogy is comparable to the Lord, *the light,* conversing with Moses from the midst of the burning bush in Sinai.

To quell the sense of foreboding that troubled Moses, God empowered his "shepherd's staff" with authority – a simile for the "staff of Life" that accompanies the Word's second reading. This he was to use in executing God's judgments against Pharaoh. For the Lord assured Moses, "I will bring Israel out of Egypt by great judgments and with a mighty hand. You shall be as a god to Pharaoh and your brother, Aaron, shall be your prophet."

After Moses had returned to Egypt, he assembled his brethren and relayed to them all that was revealed to him in the mount, and they believed him. As messengers sent from God, Moses and Aaron then appeared before Pharaoh, saying, "The Lord God of Israel sends this Word to you; LET MY PEOPLE GO, THAT THEY MAY MAKE A FEAST TO ME IN THE WILDERNESS." But Pharaoh would not let Israel go.

Upon reviewing Pharaoh's repeated refusals to bow to God's authority, twelve in all, and the consequent judgments brought against Egypt, what stands out above all else is the working of a reciprocal law, a law that prescribed that with what measure Pharaoh, *the faculty of Reason,* judged it would be measured to him. ("With what measure you judge it shall be measured to you.") Since the faculty of Reason is "a house divided against itself," it followed that, as Pharaoh's wrath against Israel mounted, the plagues brought upon Egypt worsened. By the time Egypt had suffered its eleventh judgment, the land was in ruins.

Nonetheless, Israel was spared from Egypt's tribulation. In the eleventh hour, while the angel of death passed over all the land and all the firstborn of Egypt died, the Hebrew people prepared a feast of "Passover."

They took sustenance from within their houses and ate unleavened bread, *unraised bread,* and prepared a lamb from their father's house, *signifying the lamb of God,* placing the blood of the lamb, *the light of Life,* upon the three pillars of every door, as prescribed by God. The symbols of God's presence within the house thus spared their lives.

After the destroyer had passed through Egypt, Pharaoh consented to letting Israel go. On that day the children of God departed into the desert, taking with them all the wealth of Egypt they could carry. Their multitude numbered six hundred thousand, plus a great host of others that accompanied them. They came from the east and west, from the cities and the countryside, and journeyed into the wilderness until they came to the sea, *the SEE,* that ran through the midst of the wilderness.

Meanwhile, Pharaoh's anger exploded into a change of heart, and he ordered his armies to pursue and destroy Israel. When the outcasts saw a great cloud of dust on the horizon and Pharaoh's host bearing down on them, they feared for their lives. But Moses calmed the multitude. Stretching forth his staff over the sea, he called upon the name of the Lord, saying, "BEHOLD, THE SALVATION OF GOD!" And the waters of the sea parted to the right and to the left, and the children of Israel passed through the mirroring waters on dry ground.

Believing they could do the same, Pharaoh and his host pursued Israel into the midst of the divided sea, *into the midst of that knowledge which divided the temporal mind from Israel's quasi-spiritual instruction.* But the waters of the sea, *the SEE,* that allowed Israel safe passage closed upon Pharaoh, and the strength of Egypt perished. God's twelfth judgment thus consumed Pharaoh, *the house of temporal Reason,* with all the armies that followed him.

Rejoicing over their salvation, the people sang praises unto their God, for his judgments against Egypt and for their deliverance from the oppressor. Nevertheless, as they continued their journey toward Sinai the Lord tried them. They grew weary from the long trek and began murmuring against Moses, considering how they might have been better off to stay in Egypt.

In the third month following their departure from Egypt's dark land, they came to the wilderness of Sinai. There they camped before the mount of God to await further instruction. ("They that wait upon the Lord shall renew their strength; they shall mount up with wings as eagles; they shall run and not be weary; and they shall walk and not faint.") For a second time, Moses ascended Sinai to converse with God and be directed on how Israel should proceed.

Israel and the Law of Life

"I will declare the decree: The Lord said to me, You are my Son; this day I have begotten you."

PSALMS 2:7

When God conversed with Moses in Sinai, he referred to Israel as "My beloved Son, my firstborn." This tells us that in choosing Israel to play the role of his firstborn witness, *his external witness*, the quasi-spiritual was to serve as the forerunner of his second-born witness, *his spiritual witness*. With the exodus of Abraham's seed from Egypt and their arrival at Sinai, the Lord's "firstborn" was now by his side.

Since Moses had brought Israel to the mount of God to receive further instruction, we must assume their introduction to the "second-born" was imminent; that the quasi-spiritual mind was about to be spiritualized. The time had come for Israel's glory in the Lord to be revealed.

It is important to note that although the quasi-spiritual and the spiritual proceed from a common source, they are vastly different. In the quasi-spiritual, the invisible is made visible; Spirit is translated into substance. In the spiritual, the visible is made invisible; substance is translated into Spirit – similar to the translating of visible Creation into invisible thought. Prior to their arrival at Sinai, God had witnessed to Israel only through outpictured "signs and wonders," conveying his presence through quasi-spiritual events. But now he was about to reveal to his people what they had seen only from afar, namely the presence of his Spirit within form. Through the mind's inherent ability to convert, Israel's quasi-spiritual knowledge was about to be raised to a higher level of comprehension, providing them with a true spiritual reality. ("I am your exceeding great reward.")

It is clear that the multitude that escaped from Egypt and arrived at Sinai failed to understand their higher calling; for while Moses was on the mount receiving instruction, the children of Israel were busy fashioning an idol from the gold they had taken from Egypt. Returning to the idolatrous customs of the Egyptians, they molded a "golden calf" and, bowing to its authority, they began celebrating its power. Listening to the counsel of temporal Reason, they rejected the promises God had made to Abraham and chose idolatry over true judgment. ("They changed their glory into the likeness of an ox.")

When Moses came down from the mount carrying the two tablets containing God's spiritual instruction, knowledge that would lead to Israel's promised inheritance, and saw the people had fashioned a golden calf, he was enraged. He cast the tablets to the ground and God's spiritual covenant with his "firstborn" was broken. Moses then took the golden calf, broke it into pieces, and stamped its fragments into the dust. When Moses returned to the mount to accept the consequences for their transgression, God provided him with a second set of instructions. But these were not the same as the first. The words inscribed upon the two stone tablets were "interpretive." Each inscription embodied a linear and a parallel reading, a "quickening law" that rewarded every man according to his works. ("I shall give to every man according to his works.")

Serving as Israel's mirror, these enigmatic inscriptions became man's judge and jury. When they were conceived as externally oriented, man's knowledge became externally oriented; when they were conceived as internally oriented, man's knowledge became internally oriented. ("With what measure you judge it shall be measured to you.") This transposing of the law is illustrated as follows:

- To the temporal mind, the law of Moses was a book of commands and ordinances to be performed in a literal manner. The mind's judgmental reward was determined by its earthy perceptions.
- To the quasi-spiritual mind, the law was a document of promise, a foretelling of the coming of things not seen. The mind's judgmental reward was determined by its obedience to those perceptions.
- To the spiritual mind, the law was a portal that opened into the kingdom of heaven; a mirror wherein it beheld its true spiritual identity. The mind's judgmental reward was determined by the Unity that accompanied those perceptions.

Christ identified himself with the law's spiritual aspect when he said, "I have come not to destroy the law and the prophets, but to fulfill them." And he chided the Jews, saying, "If you had believed Moses you would have known me; for Moses spoke of me." The mind of Christ is therefore recognized as the spiritual fulfillment of the law. As the prophet Hosea relates, "In the third day, *in the mind's third level of comprehension,* he shall raise us up."

God's purpose in providing Israel with the law's reciprocal judgment was, as Christ said, "To seek and to save that which was lost"; namely temporal and quasi-spiritual cognizance. From the very beginning, man failed to understand the consequences of his actions. The law's intent was to convert the mind and bring it to a higher form of judgment. It was not unlike the ladder that Jacob saw that reached all the way to heaven. Christ used the same comparison when he said, "You shall see the angels of heaven ascending and descending upon the Son of man."

With the events that transpired at Sinai, man's future was changed forever. Prior to receiving the law, man was not held spiritually accountable for his actions. Paul refers to this absence of accountability when he says, "Death reigned from Adam until Moses." However, with the advent of the word of the law, the mantle of responsibility was passed from God to man; for the law dictated that a man's reward would correspond to the thoughts of his heart. Israel's spiritual future was now to be determined by their thoughts and actions. Therefore, the kingdom of God, *the spiritual Promised Land,* would not appear until the will of God was done within man's heart as it was done in God's heaven. Today, that rule applies equally to both Jew and Gentile.

With the imparting of the Father's spiritual authority to the law, the power to outpicture manifestation was passed from Father to Son. A new form of judgment was thus introduced to mankind. Whereas God's Spirit was previously revealed through outpictured "signs and wonders," now man's spirit would be revealed through outpictured "signs and wonders." What Israel would experience was reflective of the reciprocal judgments that were brought upon Pharaoh's Egypt. As it was with Pharaoh, so would it be with Israel. With what measure they judged, it would be measured to them. Therefore, with what measure Israel afflicted the law they would likewise be afflicted. Nonetheless, the symbolism embodied in the law was, as Paul rightly expressed it, "our schoolmaster to bring us to Christ."

Although Christian theology teaches that when Christ is received, man is no longer subject to the law, Jesus taught no such thing. Indeed, Christianity's limited understanding of the law's spiritual content is proof that its reciprocal activity continues unabated. Remembering that Christ said, "All of the law and the prophets spoke of me," when we dismiss the "Word" of the law we dismiss Christ ("the Word made flesh"), and when we dismiss Christ we make the Word of God of non-effect. ("Why do you go about to kill me?")

Giving voice to the law's reciprocal principle, Christ related, "As the Father has life in himself, so has he given to the Son to have life in himself." He thus confirmed the passing of judgmental responsibility from God to man. Drawing attention to the law's all-inclusive nature, Christ informed the Jews: "You shall give account for every word that proceeds out of your mouth. With what measure you judge, it shall be measured to you." Alluding to the spiritual content of the law that signified Christ, he affirmed, "The words that I speak are Spirit and they are Life." He thus makes it clear that all judgment is subject to the law's jurisdiction. ("What you bind in earth shall be bound in heaven; and what you release in earth shall be released in heaven.") As Moses told Israel, "The Word of the Lord, *the law of the Lord,* is very near to you; even in your mouth."

When man's superficial understanding of the law is closely examined, we inevitably confront what is perceived as "the wrath of God." However, attributing man's pain to God's wrath contradicts the teachings of Christ. He explicitly told his followers to "BLESS AND CURSE NOT." We should understand that the law was not intended to be man's adversary. Rather, it was to be his "deliverer"! What the law reflects is man's adversarial attitude. The "wrath of the law" is a visible expression of the wrath embodied within the temporal mind. Knowing that self-affliction could only be overcome by a change in man's attitude, *Be it unto you according to your attitude,* Christ instructed the multitude: "Bless them that curse you. Do good unto them that despitefully use you and persecute you, that you may be the children of your Father in heaven; for he makes his sun to rise on the good and the evil and he sends his rain upon the just and the unjust."

Lamenting the wrath Israel inflicted upon God's work by transgressing the law, Isaiah wrote, "He, *the law's spiritual content,* was wounded for our transgressions, he was bruised for our iniquities. All we like sheep have gone astray; we have turned every one to his own way; and the Lord has laid on him the iniquity of us all." How wonderful it would be if we could all say time and understanding had healed that ancient wound – but that would not be true. The more things change, the more they stay the same. Appearances may vary, but the principles God has placed within his work shall remain forever.

13

Israel in the Wilderness

"All the day long I held out my hands to
a rebellious people who walked in a way
that was not good, after their own
thoughts."

ISAIAH 65:2

The Bible's account of Israel in the wilderness of
Sinai is a historical simile that reflects the
temporal experience of every man, woman and
child born into the world since time began. It is where
man's journey through life begins and, not infrequently,
ends. Though the wilderness experience is often painful,
it is an important part of man's ongoing evolution:
through the darkness of those days, a foundation is laid
for the light that follows.

The wilderness account symbolizes man's journey
through the desert of Sinai, *SIGN-"I"*. It depicts the soul
in bondage, giving visibility to the invisible powers and
principalities that subvert the mind. To emerge from
the conflict of those temporal forces is to successfully
complete the wilderness journey. The Promised Land

then comes into view and entry into the Ultimate Reality is assured.

Because Israel failed to understand that it was God's Spirit that gave them life ("Do you not know that you are the temple of God and that the Spirit of God dwells in you?"), the Lord said to Moses, "Let them build me a sanctuary, *a replica of the "true light" that was accorded man,* that I may dwell among them." Moses complied, raising THE TABERNACLE IN THE WILDERNESS. Conforming to the mind's threefold identity, the sanctuary's exterior was overlaid with skins, *symbolizing man's temporal nature.* The interior was then divided into three separate enclosures, *depicting the mind's three levels of reality, and each enclosure was veiled from the others by curtains,* signifying the psyche's three separate levels of comprehension.

Further displaying man's threefold identity, the first enclosure, with its entryway, was open to the entire congregation, *as an expression of temporal thought.* This area was called "the court of the women." The second enclosure, *as an expression of quasi-spiritual thought,* was accessible only to the ministering priests. Here, the priests interceded for the people. This area was called "the holy place." The third enclosure signified the dwelling place of "the Most High" and only the "high priest" could enter therein, *expressing spiritual thought.* This third area was called THE HOLY OF HOLIES. The psalmist speaks of this "Most Holy Place" when he writes, "He that dwells in the secret place of the Most High shall abide under the shadow of the Almighty."

Since the priesthood served as the provider of incense, *IN-SENSE,* a Golden Censor stood at the entryway to the third enclosure. Immediately beyond this third entryway, within the HOLY OF HOLIES, rested the Ark of the Covenant. The Ark was overlaid with pure gold, within and without, and served as a resting place for the Lord's testimony. The testimony within the Ark was conveyed through three spiritual symbols, each symbol witnessing to the law of Life that was embodied within God's instructional work.

The Ark's first witness was the Word of the Lord written in stone, represented by the two tablets inscribed with the Ten Commandments. ("If you keep my commandments the Father and I shall come and make our abode with you.") The Ark's second witness was Aaron's rod that had budded, representing the quasi-spiritual staff of the priesthood. ("Of all that the Father has given me I have lost nothing; and I shall raise it up again at the last day.") The Ark's third witness was the Golden Pot of Manna, *the food of angels*, that appeared on the desert rock and was gathered when the sun arose. ("I am that bread that comes down from heaven that a man may eat thereof and not die.") These three witnesses perpetually confirmed the conjunctive principle that related man to God. ("If you had believed Moses you would have known me; for Moses spoke of me.")

As the guardians of God's way, two cherubim, *two angels*, standing face-to-face overshadowed the Ark's covering, signifying the law's twofold witness: the one witnessing to the other. The "mercy seat," *the throne of God*, appeared between the cherubim, *between their symbolisms*. This was the image and likeness of the Lord's presence within the Ark, and all was overlaid with precious gold.

Each day while the craftsmen of Israel were laboring to complete their work on the sanctuary, Moses went up into the cloud that overshadowed Sinai and conversed with God. Once the work of the craftsmen was completed, the cloud of the Lord moved from atop the mount and came to rest over the tabernacle. Abstractly, the Lord dwelt in the midst of his people. Thereafter, when the cloud of his presence abode upon the tabernacle, *when the similes that signified his presence were clouded by temporal thought,* the people camped in the desert. But when the cloud was lifted from off the tabernacle, *when the similes were unveiled,* Israel resumed journeying toward the Promised Land. By day, they traveled in the shadow of his cloud, and by night they journeyed in the light of his fire. ("Your Word, O Lord, is a light unto my path, a lamp unto my feet.") However, because of their rebellious nature, the children of Israel wandered in the wilderness of Sinai for forty years before successfully entering the Promised Land.

Keeping in mind that man is a work in progress, as Israel made its nomadic way through the wilderness of Sinai, the Ark of God was carried upon the shoulders of men. This relates to all men carrying the Ark of God, *the Word similes of God,* within themselves.

Using the Ten Commandments housed inside the Ark as an example, they are diversely interpreted by mankind in the examples below.

The temporal mind views God's law as a personal charge it is obliged to keep. In performing that charge, man must do the following:

- He must love his neighbor as himself.
- He must not commit adultery.
- He must not bear false witness.
- He must not kill his own kind.

The temporal mind thus assumes charge of its own destiny.

The quasi-spiritual mind views God's law as a promised reward for services rendered. To receive that reward, man must serve as the Word's advocate. He therefore stands on the promises of God:

- He teaches that all men should love their neighbor as their self.
- He teaches that it is wrong to commit adultery.
- He teaches that it is wrong to bear false witness.
- He teaches that it is wrong to kill one's fellow man; it is injurious to the soul.

The quasi-spiritual mind thus assumes charge of its destiny and patiently awaits its reward.

The spiritual mind views God's law as an extension of itself. ("All that the Father has are mine.") Having freely received of God's Spirit, man freely gives.

- He loves his neighbor as himself – *for he knows that all of life dwells in unity and that he belongs to the continuous whole.*
- He will not adulterate – *for he beholds himself in all that is eternally true.* ("I am the truth.")

○ He will not bear false witness – *for he cannot deny himself.* ("I am the Way.")
○ He will not kill – *for he is given to the Spirit of Life.* ("I am the life.")

Because the Spiritual mind lives by virtue of eternal principles, the "true light" within the law embraces the "true light" within the man, and God becomes all in all.

The veiling that sets these three states of reality apart is comparable to the "cloud" that overshadowed the dwelling place of the Lord. As Scripture relates, "Behold, he comes with clouds," *he comes with reflective imagery.* Thus, when Christ was taken up from the earth, his disciples witnessed that "A cloud received him up out of their sight." All is symbolically expressed and, as the inheritor of those expressions, all things are found in man. ("Therefore, let no man glory in men for all things are yours; for you are Christ's; and Christ is God's.")

As our study of the mind's three states of reality progresses, the evolution of thought becomes increasingly evident. In its own way, each level of reality provides a foundation for the one to follow. Without exception, we are fellow sojourners on life's eternal path. Man's passage through the wilderness of sign "I" becomes an inextricable part of his evolution. Nevertheless, recognizing God's Spirit as man's eternal source of identity is of major importance. Hopefully, mankind's understanding of what constitutes "God's living Word" and "life eternal" will one day change.

14

The Promised Land

"The Lord took Moses up into a high place overlooking all the land of Canaan; even unto the sea. And he said to Moses, This is the land I promised I would give to Abraham's seed. I have allowed you to see it with your eyes but you shall not enter therein."

DEUTERONOMY 34:4

I n studying Israel's entry into the Promised Land, the topography and the events that attended their occupation mirrored their ongoing quasi-spiritual relationship with God. What Israel experienced in the Promised Land was a further outpicturing of the symbolism that first appeared in God's "signs and wonders" and later in the law of Moses. It also laid a foundation for future events, for that approaching day when the Lord would dwell among the nations. Though unforeseen at the time, Israel was destined to become "a light unto the Gentiles." Moses, on the other hand, would have no part in this venture. Since he knew God face-to-face, he was forbidden entry into Israel's quasi-spiritual inheritance. With the entry of Abraham's seed into the Promised Land, the labors of Moses ended. Moses walked with God throughout his days and was gathered unto the Father's Spirit.

In keeping with the previously established pattern, Israel's first attempt at entering the Promised Land failed. When the generations that departed from Egypt approached the borders of Canaan, they sent spies from each tribe to search out the countryside. When the spies returned with reports of Canaan's strength, Israel's leadership "reasoned" that their resources were insufficient to conquer the land. Joshua and Caleb – who had also gone as spies into Canaan – tried to convince the children of Israel otherwise, but they failed.

Bowing to their fears and retreating from their faith in God, the multitude returned to the wilderness of Sinai. There, every adult that had dwelt in Egypt perished, but their children were spared, as were these three men: Joshua, Caleb and Moses. Thus, from Israel's exodus from Egypt until their "Second Coming" to the Promised Land, forty years were consumed. Nevertheless, upon their return to their promised inheritance, they passed over Jordan and began their conquest of Canaan.

Dividing this "land that flowed with milk and honey" from the wilderness of Sinai is the river Jordan. The river Jordan, called "The Descender," holds special significance because of its symbolic character. The river Jordan is formed by "three streams" that come together to create a small body of water. This symbolic "lake" is four miles long and rises seven feet above sea level, *SEE level*. The highest stream feeding the lake issues from "the mouth" of a cave that is 1,000 feet above sea level. Then, joined by two additional streams, it flows twelve miles before entering the lake. The three streams and the small lake supply the upper Jordan, which begins seven feet above sea level and quickly descends below sea level. It flows approximately ten miles before forming a second lake, the quasi-spiritual Sea of Galilee, which is about twelve miles long and 682 feet below sea level.

Entrance to the lower Jordan begins at the southern end of the Sea of Galilee and runs an erratic course through Canaan until it enters the Dead Sea, 1,292 feet below sea level. It is noteworthy that the Jordan, which begins as a spring of fresh water issuing from within the earth, culminates in a sea of death, *the "Dead Sea."* What begins as fresh water, above sea level, quickly descends into salt water, below sea level.

Because the Jordan compliments the Word's instructional nature, it is frequently spoken of in symbolic terms. For instance, Elisha instructed Naaman, a captain of the host of Syria, to wash seven times in the Jordan as a cure for his leprosy. Confirming the Jordan's healing symbolism, the psalmist writes, "There is a river, the streams thereof make glad the city of God; the holy place of the tabernacles of the Most High." Also as a prelude to Christ's introducing the kingdom of God, the followers of John were baptized in the waters of the Jordan, the waters that signified their descent into quasi-spiritual death.

Since God's indwelling presence was conveyed through outpictured symbolism, Israel's passage over the Jordan set the stage for new quasi-spiritual similitudes. In preparation for their crossing, the people went through the prescribed ritual for purification. Then, instructed by God, Joshua chose one man from each tribe to participate in the ceremonial activities. At the appointed hour, the priests bearing the Ark entered the Jordan until its waters covered their feet, *covered their understanding,* for at harvest time, the waters of the Jordan overflowed all their banks. Once the ARK OF THE TESTIMONY was in place, the Jordan's descending flow stopped and "the waters stood in a heap." Joshua then took twelve stones from the riverbed and placed them, as stepping-stones, where the feet of the priests stood as they held the Ark. Those twelve stones remain in place to this day. Then, while the priests carrying the Ark stood fast, the children of Israel crossed over on dry land.

Once their crossing was complete, the twelve men chosen from among the tribes gathered twelve large stones from the river. Carrying them upon their shoulders, they placed the stones where Israel was to camp for the night. When that was accomplished, the priests bearing the Ark concluded their crossing. Thus, with the passing of Abraham's seed through the waters of the Jordan, God's Spirit was symbolically portrayed as entering into the Promised Land.

With the advent of Israel's promised inheritance, a new form of quasi-spiritual instruction emerged. Whereas Moses had provided those who came out of Egypt with a quickening law to reflect the mind's quasi-spiritual nature, this new form of instruction would use the characteristics of the Promised Land to reflect the body's quasi-spiritual nature. With the uniting of mind and body as related quasi-spiritual entities, *as one but appearing separately,* Israel's inheritance was referred to by the prophet Isaiah as Beulah. ("The married land.") God's "signs and wonders" thus received an additional quasi-spiritual witness.

Using the Promised Land as a natural parallelism for conveying the human condition required a vehicle that symbolically expressed the attributes of both God and man. That vehicle is referred to when the psalmist writes, "We found it in the field of the wood." That is, they recognized the Promised Land as being the mirror image of Eden's Paradise Garden, and the "Tree of Life" in the midst of the garden as having its place in man. Since the "signs and wonders" that appeared in the Promised Land were inherent to man, the path for their being transposed into the psyche had to pass through the eye. The Promised Land, the Tree of Life, and the human eye were thus recognized as conjunctive entities; diverse forms of instructional symbolism that God had provided to direct the psyche concerning its eternal heritage.

Jesus identified the role assigned to the eye when he said, "The light of the body is the eye, *the I,* If your eye, *your I,* is single your whole body will be full of light, but if your eye is darkened your whole body shall be darkened." The "eye" is thus referred to as "the mirror of the soul." From a spiritual viewpoint, the "I" within the faculty of vision is commensurate to the "I" within the faculty of speech. Herein, God's visible and invisible witnesses within the body are outpictured for all to see. It is noteworthy that without two eyes, *a second "I,"* man would be without depth perception. The law of Moses and Israel's occupation of the Promised Land likewise provided that perception.

Once Israel had successfully crossed the Jordan the people moved inland and camped at Gilgal – the location where the twelve stones taken from the river had been placed. The next day, the Lord gave the children of Israel a sign, saying, "Today, I have rolled away the stone of your reproach." Gilgal, "the rolling," was thereby identified as "the sight" that would serve as an additional symbol of God's presence. Thereafter, the manna Israel had eaten in the wilderness ceased and they began to eat the fruits of the land.

With the confirmation of the eye's symbolism at Gilgal, the entry of God's light through darkness became applicable to the whole of the Promised Land. Serving as a conjunction between the Promised Land and the human psyche, the eye inherited all things. Scripture therefore translates as follows:

- "Every eye shall see him; they also that pierced him. And all nations shall weep because of him."
- "To him that overcomes I will give a white stone; and in the stone a new name written."
- "Be mindful of the light that shines in a dark place."
- "Behold, a whirlwind came out of the north; a great cloud and a fire enfolding itself."
- "If you see me when I am taken up, a double portion of my spirit will be upon you; and Elijah was taken up in a whirlwind."
- "The cloud of the Lord overshadowed the tabernacle."
- "And two cherubim were placed above, on the covering of the Ark of the Testimony."

When Scripture relates, "He reveals his secret to his servants the prophets," the Word's revelation includes God's spiritual appearance in speech and vision.

The Promised Land was not to come without a price. In keeping with the voidal principle, Israel was challenged to "go in and subdue the land."

Their greatest achievements were realized under the leadership of David, "the shepherd king." David's accomplishments were astounding. Leading his armies he conquered his adversaries – and in defeating his enemies, he brought great wealth to his nation. With that wealth, he commissioned Solomon to build the temple at Jerusalem. When the work on that great edifice was completed, it was the most extravagant and glorious of its time. Yet, David would not be remembered for the battles he had won nor for the tabernacle he had raised in God's name, but for his literary contributions. God conversed with David, just as he had conversed with Moses, and David recorded those conversations in song.

Today, some three thousand years after his reign, the Psalms of David are cherished throughout the world, and men glory in their truth and beauty. Perhaps his heritage was not what he expected when God said, "There shall not fail me a man to sit upon the throne of David." Nevertheless, in all generations, men rise to the Spirit that inspired David and there, with him, sit upon his throne.

To say that David was an enigma in his own time would be an understatement. While contributing to the welfare of his people, he simultaneously foresaw their approaching quasi-spiritual demise. This was indicated when he said, "The stone that the builders refused, *the quasi-spiritual truth they refused to build upon,* has become the headstone of the corner." Relating to this insight he questioned God, "What is man that you are mindful of him; and the Son of man that you visit him?" Little did he realize that the Son of man would one day appear as the Christ, as man's "Deliverer."

Following David's victorious and prophetic reign, and the subsequent reign of his son, King Solomon, Israel's decline began. Israel's disregard for God's "signs and wonders" in their Promised Land culminated in the destruction of Jerusalem and the burning of the House of God. Those who were spared from the wrath of Nebuchadnezzar's armies were taken into captivity. Having lost their inheritance, they descended into Babylon, and were scattered amongst the nations. Yet, as captive exiles, they served God's purpose for they became "a light unto the Gentiles."

The Age of the Prophets

"Unto us a child is born, unto us a Son is given; and the government of the people shall be upon his shoulders. And his name shall be called Wonderful, Counselor, the Mighty God, the Everlasting Father, the Prince of Peace."

ISAIAH 9:6

Without an end there can be no beginning; without death there can be no resurrection. Consequently, Israel's loss of the Promised Land ushered in a great new era: the Age of the prophets. God's "signs and wonders" in Israel had finally born spiritual fruit. Now, for the first time, men were looking into the Word of the law and beholding their faces as in a glass. It was a momentous occasion, and the prophets heralded what they saw as their rebirth into the Son of man. ("Son of man, stand upon your feet and I will speak to you.")

As the forerunner and symbol of this new Age, the prophet Elijah was translated into heaven; and as benefactors of his translation, the Spirit of Elijah rested upon all the prophets. However, the Age of the prophets ended with the beheading of John the Baptist. As Jesus confirmed: "The law and the prophets were until John. Now the kingdom of God is preached."

Relating to the circumstances surrounding Elijah's translation, Elisha was asked if he had a last request before his master was taken from him. In reply, Elisha asked to receive a double portion of Elijah's Spirit. "You ask a hard thing," said Elijah, "but if you see me when I am taken up, a double portion of my spirit, *AN UNDERSTANDING OF THE WORD'S TWO WITNESSES,* shall be upon you." And it was so. There appeared horses of fire and a chariot of fire, *words of fire and truths of fire,* and Elijah was taken up in a whirlwind, *in a spiritual countercurrent.*

In the process of Elijah's translation, his *quasi-spiritual* mantle fell from him and Elisha picked it up. He took the mantle to the river Jordan and with it he smote the waters, crying, "Where is the Lord God of Elijah?" And the waters were parted so that Elisha passed over on dry land. The quasi-spiritual Jordan thus responded to the spiritual authority imparted to Elijah's mantle at the time of his ascent. The passing of Elijah's Spirit to Elisha, and to all the prophets who followed, was thereby confirmed.

Some nine hundred years later, the Son of man, to whom all of the law and the prophets witnessed, would take three of his disciples and ascend onto the "Mount of Transfiguration." There, he would converse with Moses and Elijah. The coming together of these three in COMMON-UNION portends to the approaching hour when the Holy Ghost, *the embodied Spirit of the Son of man,* would be introduced to the world.

Of course, the motivating factor behind the rise of the prophets was Israel's loss of their quasi-spiritual Promised Land and, more directly, the loss of their faith in God. The fact that God found it necessary to void his first covenant with Israel can be attributed to the truth that Israel had already made void his covenant through idolatry. Once again, the law of cause and effect came into play. Israel had sown the wind, *what was temporal and void of all truth,* and reaped the whirlwind, *the quasi-spiritual "signs and wonders" they had made void of all truth.* ("He that leads into captivity shall go into captivity. He that kills with the sword, *of truth,* shall be killed by the sword, *of truth.*") Notwithstanding, the Spirit of God remained with the prophets and, as in the beginning, they began filling the void with light. To once again give spiritual substance to his work, God provided Israel with a second covenant. The prophets, having experienced a deep sense of personal loss through Israel's captivity, *a void within themselves,* now cried unto the Lord. From the midst of their anguish and emptiness the light of God's new covenant emerged, the light of the Son of man.

Isaiah defines God's relationship to the Son of man and his preordained mission when he writes:

"I, the Lord, have called you, *the Son of man,* in righteousness. I will hold your hand and keep you. My covenant shall be in you, giving light to the darkness.

Through you, I shall bring the blind by a way they have not known. I will lead

> them in paths where they have not
> walked. I will turn darkness into light
> before them and crooked things I shall
> make straight."

Introduced to Israel as "The Arm of the Lord," the Son of man thus entered into the prophets, and in him they were glorified.

Since the prophets now recognized God's work as a personal parallelism, Jeremiah interpreted the destruction of Jerusalem and the burning of the House of God as indicative of the mind's quasi-spiritual failure. From personal experience, he understood that as a prerequisite to God's new covenant, the old covenant had to end. Mirroring that conclusion, he wrote, "For as long as the land, *the quasi-spiritual mind,* lay desolate, she, *the spiritual mind,* kept Sabbath." He thus discloses the key to the prophets' spiritual quickening, the key that lay hidden in the ruins of Jerusalem. This principle resurfaces at Christ's crucifixion when he tells the Jews, "Behold, your house is left unto you desolate; and you shall not see me from henceforth until you say, Blessed is he that comes in the name of the Lord."

Perhaps the greatest wonder ever realized by man was the revelation that all the works of God came alive in the Son of man. ("He that overcomes shall inherit all things.") The law of Moses, the sojourn in the wilderness of Sinai, the events that transpired in the Promised Land, even the principles that shaped heaven and earth, all conformed to man's new identity. ("I will write upon him my new name, which is THE WORD OF GOD.") Yet the prophets of Israel found their position untenable and confessed, "they were strangers in a land that was not theirs."

Although the quickening of the Son of man had spiritualized the mind, the body remained captive to its temporal nature, *outpictured as Israel's captivity amongst the Gentiles.* Looking forward to the day when the body would be spiritualized and freed from earthy servitude, Isaiah wrote, "I am the voice of one crying in the wilderness, Prepare a way for the Lord; make straight in the desert a highway for our God." Much later, as the forerunner of Christ's spiritualized body, *the Word made flesh,* John told the Jews, "He that comes after me is preferred before me, because he was before me."

In studying the advent of the Son of man an explanation of his origin is in order. While Paul writes, "The first man is of the earth, earthy, the second man is the Lord from heaven," he does not provide a foundation for understanding the Son of man's origin. Jesus, on the other hand, emphasized the importance of origin. He explained, "That born of the flesh is flesh and that born of the Spirit is Spirit." Not to be misunderstood, he added, "Flesh and blood cannot inherit the kingdom of God." His emphasis on origin brings us closer to understanding how differences in "birthing" affect man. Understandably, that born of the flesh proceeds from an earthy source while that born of the Spirit proceeds from a spiritual source. These two points of origin are vastly different; the earthy witnesses to the "ever-changing," the spiritual witnesses to the "never-changing."

As portrayed by Genesis, Adam was formed from the dust of the ground and his personality evolved through the senses. Conversely, the Son of man originated in the Father; and his character evolved, as the Father's true light. ("The light of Life.") Since the "light of Life" is embodied in all mankind, providing his entire frame with sensory reality, we have only to "void" the mind's sensory misconceptions and its "true light" will shine forth. ("Judge not according to the appearance but judge right judgment.") With the psyche's renewal, the Son of man is received and the Word of truth that appears at his coming nurtures all. Unlike the first man, the Son of man proceeds directly from God and is alike to God. Embodied in man as God's living Word, he continues to evolve as "the brightness of the Father's glory and the express image of his person."

This brings us to a clarification of what Christ implied when he told the Jews, "You must be born again." While it is true that "belief" is a prelude to rebirth, once rebirth is accomplished "belief" is passed away. The Son of man does not "believe" anything. He knows; and he knows that he knows. The Father meets all of his needs. He *is* not waiting for life eternal. He is life eternal. Through him, the FINITE leaps into the INFINITE.

Further relating to the mind's spiritual rebirth, because the kingdom of God exists as a parallelism, all linear thought must be "born again," *must be spiritually clothed upon.* Since Judeo-Christian doctrine is "clouded" by linear misconceptions, it, too, must be "born again." Remember, the mind becomes the servant of what it serves. Christ referred to the shortcomings of linear knowledge when he told the Hebrew priests, "You shall see Abraham, Isaac and Jacob, and all the prophets, set down in the kingdom of God, *appearing as quasi-spiritual parallelisms,* but you yourselves shall be thrust out."

Generation after generation has succumbed to the misconceptions of linear "belief" and, as a result, religious division abounds. Today, the muffled voices of the prophets are heard but few respond. As past masters of Israel's history, their words are distanced from the present. Yet in the mind of The Eternal, nothing changes. Like the prophets of old, each generation is called upon to make straight the crooked places. Each generation is challenged to prepare in the desert a highway for our God. Individually, we are a work in progress, and although "the harvest is great, the laborers are few."

16

The Prophets and the End Time

"Arise! Shine! For the light has come; and the glory of the Lord has risen upon you. The Gentiles shall come to your light, and kings to the brightness of your rising."

ISAIAH 60:3

With the demise of Israel as a nation, the spiritual reward of God's law dawned as morning light over the Promised Land. Israel's loss of its quasi-spiritual inheritance not only gave birth to its higher calling, but also presented the world with an unforeseen opportunity. With the scattering of Abraham's seed among the nations, Israel now became "a light unto the Gentiles." Their captivity had prepared the way for extending God's glory throughout the entire earth. All nations now became potential benefactors of the Word's redeeming light.

To bring Israel's captivity into perspective, we must return to the mind's three states of reality. Having undergone the transition of a new covenant, Israel, a quasi-spiritual people – and the Gentiles – a temporal people – were now recognized as "being of one mind." They two were made one flesh. In this new scenario, the prophets, having received the spiritual mind of the Son of man, now assumed the role of God's "Way-shower." They proceeded with that task by providing spiritual seed for both Israel and the Gentiles. However, because of the mind's conflicting levels of comprehension, the success of their labors would be extremely limited. Until the attitude that voided God's counsel was removed, the light they were bringing into the world would not shine out of darkness. Israel's captivity amongst the Gentiles thus signaled the beginning of what history records as the disastrous "end time"; an era referred to by the Book of Revelation as "the great tribulation."

That chaotic period actually began in the Promised Land, when the children of Israel turned away from keeping the law of Moses and started adopting the idolatrous practices of the Gentiles. In adopting their abominations, the quasi-spiritual aspect of the law of God was made of non-effect. ("You make the Word of God of non-effect by your tradition.") That "falling away" ultimately led to Israel's desolation. The prophet Daniel characterized the transgressing of God's covenant by his people as THE ABOMINATION THAT MAKES DESOLATE. Jesus agreed with that assessment, advising his followers: "When you shall see the abomination that makes desolate standing in the holy place, let him that is in Judea flee into the mountains, *to higher ground.* Let him that is on the housetop, *the psyche,* not come down to take anything out of his house; for then shall be great tribulation."

Christ referred to this experience when his disciples asked what to expect in "the end time." Cloaking his reply, he shaped parables to convey his message. Drawing attention to the deceptive practices that would take hold in the "end time," he warned: "Let no man deceive you by any means. Then shall be great tribulation; and except those days should be shortened, *except the days of misconception that hold the temporal and quasi-spiritual minds captive should come to an end,* there should no flesh be saved. But, for the sake of the elect, *those who have chosen God's way,* those days shall be shortened. As a light that comes out of the east and shines to the west, so shall be the coming of the Spirit of truth. When you see all these things coming to pass, know that the end is near, even at the doors."

It is important that we recognize Jerusalem's desolation as symbolic, for it provides a simile of that condition which permeates religions throughout the world. Namely, the mind set of "will worship" – the willingness to adopt practices which only enhance the mind's voidal condition. Recognition of this ongoing dilemma is a prerequisite to obtaining spiritual light. ("You cannot embrace the thoughts of God and embrace the thoughts of the temporal mind.") As the prophet affirmed: "Your ways are not my ways, said the Lord. Neither are your thoughts my thoughts."

The role of the prophets, therefore, became twofold. First, they were to instill a sense of darkness and desolation within Israel and the Gentiles. Then, they were to reconcile that darkness to the Spirit of God. These opposing tasks are demonstrated in the following passage:

"Behold, the Lord has made the earth waste. He has scattered the inhabitants and there is none spared. The land is utterly emptied and spoiled.

The inhabitants have defiled the earth. They have transgressed the laws, changed the ordinances, and broken the everlasting covenant.

Therefore, a curse has devoured the land and the inhabitants are consumed. Only a remnant remains."

After addressing man's desolation, the prophets then turn to the task of reconciliation:

"The Spirit of the Lord is upon me. He has anointed me to preach good tidings to the meek. He has sent me to bind up the brokenhearted, to proclaim liberty to the captives and the opening of the prison to them that are bound. To proclaim the acceptable year of the Lord."

Supporting the purpose behind these two seemingly contradictory messages, the prophet writes, "For all of this, the anger of the Lord is not turned away; but, his hand is outstretched still."

The Son of man restated this "end time" principle at Herod's temple in Jerusalem when he told the Jews,

"Tear down this house and in three days I will raise it up." What he said mirrored the previously stated passages and referred to the raising of the Word's spiritual aspect on the third day.

When the principle of "the end time" is closely examined, we discover the desolation of nations is based upon the consummation of all things in death. Thereafter, the mind's awareness is raised through spiritual translation. Death is then swallowed up with Life. Although the scope of events surrounding Israel's captivity obscures what it seeks to accomplish, there is no hiding the truth: "He that seeks his life must lose it." Loss of the temporal self was the centerpiece of Abraham's calling, it was the centerpiece of the law of Moses, and it was the centerpiece of Israel's inheritance in the Promised Land. It was also destined to be the centerpiece of "the end time" when the Word's quasi-spiritual essence would be crucified and mankind's spiritual inheritance in Christ would ascend to the Father. ("Where I go you cannot now come; but afterwards you shall follow.")

Why was this death-principle of such importance? Because man had to rebuild the symbolism that determined the mind's character. Only by bringing man's temporal limitations to an end could spiritual freedom be achieved. ("You shall know the truth and the truth shall make you free.") By converting quasi-spiritual symbolism to spiritual symbolism, the mind would be changed. On the other hand, changing our "beliefs" from one form of temporal or quasi-spiritual symbolism to another would defeat the whole process. This form of redirection has nothing in common with true spiritual translation. True spiritual translation witnesses to the

Father of lights, in whom there is no variableness. ("Except the Lord keep the gate, the watchman awakens but in vain.")

Perhaps the most ingenious aspect of "the end time" comes to light when the prophets begin transposing their spiritual inheritance in the Son of man into Scripture's Word. For it was through the Word of truth initiated by Moses that the prophets obtained a "first resurrection" and were spiritually raised. The concept thus followed that sowing an immortal entity into a mortal frame held the promise of providing a coexisting spiritual mind and body – the truth that a little leaven could raise the whole mass. The prophets, therefore, followed the lead of Moses and sowed quasi-spiritual interpretations into the linear aspect of God's witnessing Word hoping that, in time, their labors would culminate with a "second resurrection," *the resurrection of God's Word made flesh in man.* They were not disappointed. Immediately, however, the prophets had to contend with feelings of an immortal mind residing in a mortal body, and their spiritual predictions mirrored their predicament. As parallelisms relating to Israel's outpictured desolation, they saw the spirit of the Son of man within themselves as "the voice of one crying in the wilderness." And they labored in that wilderness to prepare a highway in the desert for their God.

The labors of the prophets therefore took on an added dimension. They needed not only to reconcile the nations to God; they also needed to reconcile the human frame to God. Thus, by translating the spiritual attributes of the Son of man into Scripture's quasi-spiritual content, the Word was made flesh – and this embodied Word was personalized with the advent of Jesus Christ.

Looking forward to the fulfilling of "the end time," when both mind and body would be spiritualized, the prophet quotes the Lord as saying:

"Behold, I shake not only the heavens, *the mind*, but the earth, *the body*, also; and the desire of all nations shall come. And I will fill this desolation with my glory.

And the glory of this latter house shall be greater than the former. In this place they shall find peace."

By this he signifies that only those things that cannot be shaken will remain. At that time, the whole earth, *mind and body*, shall be filled with knowledge of the glory of the Lord.

Until we realize that darkness and death are upon us, *to be experienced by all as the immediate forerunners of life eternal*, man will continue to live out his days in adversity, *the era of THE GREAT TRIBULATION*. Although most religions teach "life after death," their doctrinal misconceptions continue to obscure the truth. Paul envisioned death as a vehicle of transition when he wrote, "Through death, the Son of man overcame him who had the power of death"; namely the faculty of temporal Reason. Thus, with the fulfilling of "the end time," death is swallowed up with Life. This was the message trumpeted by the prophets, and this is the message the present generation must yet hear and understand. "Those who are buried with Christ in the likeness of his *quasi-spiritual* death are also raised with him in the likeness of his *spiritual* resurrection." It could not be otherwise!

The Embodied Son of Man

"This is the day that the Lord has made; we will rejoice and be glad in it."

PSALMS 118:24

With the birth of Jesus Christ, the labors of the prophets came to fruition. They had sown the Word of the Lord into the human frame, and that planted in Spirit was now reaped in Spirit. In Christ, the works of the prophets became "spiritually embodied." As John witnessed, "The Word was made flesh; and we beheld his glory as the only begotten of the Father, full of grace and truth." The Word's spiritual glory in man was now openly displayed for all to see.

In studying Christ's introduction to the world as the Son of God, we immediately confront the conjecture surrounding his origin – currently expressed in Christian doctrine as the "immaculate conception" and the "virgin birth." To the temporal mind it presented an irreconcilable enigma; a tenet that could only be accepted through "blind faith." Yet to the spiritual mind it was a miracle of God, one that expressed the glory of God and the power of God. The conjecture surrounding

Christ's birth should be resolved, and this can be done by briefly reviewing events beginning with Genesis.

In the beginning, when the invisible gave birth to the visible, *when the Spirit of God gave birth to Creation,* temporal form appeared. Then, by creating man as a sensory "in-version" of external form, the visible was transformed into the invisible – visible Creation was transformed into invisible thought. But when Adam and Eve failed to recognize the spiritual aspect of their identity, the mind, *Eve,* transgressed. She judged Creation's "Tree of Knowledge" by its appearance, and the cognizance of the first couple emerged in a temporal state. The spiritual aspect of man's inheritance was thus lost. With their future hanging in the balance, a redemptive scenario was now needed.

The key to that effort lay hidden in the pattern of Creation's internal glory, for that glory was assimilated into all of God's work. The Creator's plan for regenerating man therefore called for A RESEEDING OF THE MIND THROUGH A PARALLELING OF SIMILES THAT EXPRESSED HIS GLORY. And this was accomplished through an outpicturing of revelatory truths. This "reseeding of the mind" began with Abraham's calling, when the Patriarch was instructed to leave the place of his birth and journey into a land that God would show him. "There," said the Lord, "I will multiply your seed as the stars of heaven for multitude." The sowing of this "new seed," *THE SEED OF THE MOST HIGH,* provided the spiritual base for what is now recognized as the "immaculate conception." That is, "seed" conceived from God.

Beginning with Abraham's calling, God provided "new seed" for the Patriarch's mind. Seed that was sown in the form of outpictured "signs and wonders," through the appearing of a heavenly host. When Abraham recognized those "signs and wonders" within himself, he gave birth to a child formed of God. This is what Christ referred to when he said, "Abraham rejoiced to see my day." This was the "GOD CHILD" who was predestined to achieve man's redemption. We thus see a "new mind," *a woman untouched by man,* conceiving from God and giving birth to the Son man – outpictured as the "virgin birth" of Jesus Christ.

In that context, he that is "reborn" into the Son of man ("HE THAT HAS 'SEED' CONCEIVED FROM GOD") has the virgin birth within himself. He is born of a "new mind." He has given birth to the Son of God. ("Unto us a child is born. Unto us a Son is given.")

John's Revelation characterizes this event in the following manner:

"There appeared a great wonder in heaven. A woman clothed with the sun, and the moon under her feet; and upon her head a crown of twelve stars. And she being with child cried, travailing in birth, and pained to be delivered.

And she brought forth a man child, who was to rule all nations with a rod of iron, *a sword having two edges,* and her child was caught up unto God and to his throne."

Because John's symbolism depicts an era that encompasses the greater part of the Bible, the role played by Mary, the mother of Jesus, is seen as no more than a symbolic portrayal of God's outpictured redemptive plan.

While the birth of Jesus Christ is recognized as a fulfilling of prophecy ("I have come not to destroy the law and the prophets but to fulfill them"), it must also be viewed as an extension of God's progressive revelation. ("All things must be fulfilled that are spoken of me.") The primary function of the law and the prophets was to spiritually characterize the Son of man through "signs and wonders." Now, with the birth of Jesus, that characterization had appeared in bodily form. ("The Word was made flesh.") Jesus thus represented THE BEGINNING OF A NEW GENERATION; the first man to be spiritualized in both mind and body. ("Christ the first fruits; then, those who are Christ's at his coming.") So when the Son of man said, "Flesh and blood cannot inherit the kingdom of heaven," his intention was not to imply that his Father's kingdom was "otherworldly." ("My kingdom is not of this world.") He simply meant that his was a spiritual kingdom, not a temporal kingdom, that his was a spiritual body, not a temporal body. He therefore told his disciples, "You must eat my flesh and drink my blood, *the Word's spiritual content,* or you have no life in you."

This brings us to the resolution of two distinct "resurrections." The first is the quickening of God's Word within the mind. The second is the quickening of God's Word within the body. Since the two were now "seeded" into one body, *as the Spirit of the Son of man sown into the flesh,* Jesus was akin to the prophets. But there was one difference: The Word of the Lord sown into the flesh by the prophets had yet to be glorified.

("The Holy Ghost was not yet given in that Jesus was not yet glorified.") The need for a second glorification is restated when Christ prays, "Father, glorify your Son with your own Spirit." And God replies, "I have glorified you, *as the Son of man in the mind of the prophets,* and I will glorify you again, *as the Son of man in the flesh.*" We thus see the advent of the Holy Ghost accomplishing a "second resurrection" – the glorification of both mind and body, a glory wherein the Spirit of God is personified in the flesh. Paul witnessed to this spiritual transformation when he said, "For I know that if our earthy house were dissolved, we have a building of God, *a spiritual mind and body,* a house not made with hands, *an immaculate conception,* eternal in the heavens."

Recalling that when the prophets were sowing the Spirit of the Son of man into the flesh, Israel and the Gentiles were historically included; so it followed that the temporal "Gentiles" and the quasi-spiritual children of Abraham were counted among the least and the lost. Consequently, the nations now appeared within man as a chaotic multitude of spiritual misconceptions; a world of temporal beliefs founded upon the miscalculations of a "reasonable mind." We therefore read: "To him that *spiritually* overcomes, I will give power over the nations. As the vessels of a potter shall they be broken to shivers." But once this "breaking of the nations" is accomplished, the prophet writes, "I will turn the desire of nations toward the Spirit of the Lord and all nations shall flow into it." We thus see all nations included in God's redemptive plan, and this was made possible through the culmination of all things in one body – the body of Jesus Christ.

With the reconciling of the above and the below in the Holy Ghost ("Heaven and earth are full of his glory") a new form of judgment emerged: A judgment characterized by Christ as "the kingdom of God." Whereas in the beginning of God's revelatory work his Spirit witnessed to his presence through outpictured "signs and wonders," that process was now reversed. Through a glorified "in-version" of the body's sensory system, a knowing of spiritual truths that were previously externalized now reappeared internalized. Through this "in-version" of understanding, the glory the Son of man had with the Father "before the world was," was transposed into man. The kingdom of God was thus identified as a kingdom of spiritual knowledge and understanding, a kingdom that provided the mind with an "in-version" of life and with true judgment ("the last judgment").

Christ indicated the immediacy of obtaining God's kingdom when he told the Jews: "The kingdom of God is at hand. Therefore, seek and you shall find; knock and it shall be opened to you." He reiterated the same when he told his disciples, "You shall not have gone through the cities of Judea before the Son of man has come in his Father's kingdom." ("Behold, I come quickly.") However, as it was with Israel in that transitional Age, so it is today, "They could not enter into his kingdom because of unbelief."

When we look beyond Christ's physical appearance into the spiritual content of his body, we discover an entity formed of God; a "New Creation" wherein the Sons of God make their eternal home – a body not of another world, but a sanctuary of truth and light wherein the Father shares his eternal glory. But, as the book of Hebrews cautions, "Be watchful, lest you fail to enter into his rest; for we who truly believe do enter therein."

18

The Ministry of Christ

"For God, having reconciled Christ unto himself, has given to him, and to us, the ministry of reconciliation."

2 CORINTHIANS 5:18

To understand the ministry of Christ in macrocosm, as opposed to the limitations of time and place imposed upon Jesus the man, an overview of his spiritual character and the scope of his mission on earth are necessary. From the moment of Creation's inception, when God and his light emerged from the dark abyss, Christ, "The Arm of the Lord," assumed the role of witness and revelator. Therein, the Creator became the created and the spiritual became quasi-spiritual. ("The Father and I are one.")

Because all had issued from the dark void ("He has made his light to shine out of darkness"), God inherited two distinct natures: one of primal darkness, the other of quasi-spiritual light. And these two conditions were expressed in his work. Genesis therefore relates: "And God made two great lights, the greater light to rule the day, and the lesser light to rule the night: he made the stars also. And God set them in the firmament of the heaven to give light upon the earth."

When this analogy of the heavens' "two great lights" is transposed into the character of man, it reads as follows:

"And God imparted two great lights to the consciousness of man, His spiritual light to rule over the day and his quasi-spiritual light to rule over the night. He provided the mind with revelatory "signs and wonders," also. And he set them within the human frame to give light to man's evolving knowledge."

Keeping in mind the limitations of time and place imposed upon Scripture's analogy of how Creation was formed in seven days, we should be eminently aware that for billions of years prior to the writing of that simile, the light that emerged from the dark abyss witnessed only to the character of its primordial source. It was not until man had acquired limited sensory judgment that a base for the future evolution of thought was considered. To provide man with that judgmental base, a witness equal to the light that identified the Creator's spiritual character was required. With that capacity attained, man would then evolve with true judgment.

Since all the Works of God adhered to the principle of bringing forth after their own kind, the problem of furthering the evolution of thought was, for a short period, resolved. To satisfy that need, the Creator and his witnessing light endowed man with an array of faculties capable of creating a microcosm equal to the macrocosm of their complementary relationship. The Book of Genesis identifies this point in time with the pluralism, "Let *US* make man in *OUR* image and after *OUR* likeness." Accordingly, the correlative attributes of the Creator and his witnessing light were extended to man, providing Creation's "God-made-man" with a Self-evaluating witness. But mankind's attaining of "right judgment" was destined to be "a work in progress." The labor of bringing this newly formed parallelism to perfection began with the analogy of Adam and Eve exiting Eden, and continued for some four thousand years before reaching completion. Paul referred to the imparting of the Creator's integrity to mankind as "the secret kept from the foundation of the world, Christ, *God's light,* in us the hope of glory."

As time progressed, the Creator and his witnessing light chose the lineage of the three Patriarchs' to exemplify the inherent principles they wished to convey to the world. Through "signs and wonders," the macrocosm of God's labors in the above were mirrored into the microcosm of man's labors in the below. ("Whatsoever the Father does, the Son does likewise.") This mirroring of the Creator's attributes would continue, uninterrupted, until it had successfully reached completion. ("Father, I have finished the work that you gave me to do.")

Since life's basic tenet directs that all life must emerge from darkness before attaining "true light," it inevitably followed that the Patriarchs lineage would begin their revelatory mission by descending into

Egypt's dark land, where they would remain in captivity for four hundred years. Thereafter, they would be freed from Pharaoh's control and depart from Egypt as a newborn nation. They would then journey to Sinai, the mount of God, where Moses would identify the Creator's witnessing light in man as "The Arm of the Lord." ("Israel, my beloved Son; my firstborn.") Joined to the Word of the law, their nation would inherently acquire the Creator's regenerative ability, which committed the Patriarchs' lineage to revealing the quickening effect of the law. The thoughts of their hearts would thus materialize, bringing forth manifestation after their own kind. ("As the Father has life in himself, so has he given to the Son to have life in himself.")

After wandering in the wilderness of temporal dissention for forty years, the children of Israel would finally enter the Promised Land. The presence of "The Arm of the Lord" was thus extended to include the land of Canaan. With the acquisition of that inheritance, the land was called "Beulah," the married land. But that glorious era of time was short-lived. Giving way to quasi-spiritual infidelity, Israel would lose its inheritance and be dispersed amongst the nations. With the voiding of Israel's covenant with their God and the destruction of Jerusalem, "The Arm of the Lord" would resurface within the prophets. The quickening Life embodied within the Word of the law was, therein, identified as the Son of man. This transcending event marked a huge step forward in the light's quest to complete its revelatory work.

With the quickening of the Son of man within the prophets, God's two natures, *one of light, the other of darkness*, were then portrayed as Israel and the Gentiles. Capitalizing on that historic circumstance, the prophets began sowing these two conflicting attributes into Scripture's Word. The countless facets of truth their labors conveyed enhanced God's revelatory work and added immensely to the spiritual content of the Word's second readings. However, the Age of the prophets came to an end with the birth of Jesus of Nazareth. In him "The Arm of the Lord" was made flesh, and he assumed the role of the promised Christ. What was previously witnessed through external "signs and wonders" was now bodily transposed, witnessing internally in Spirit and in truth. Free of human error, man thus began seeing himself through the "true light" God had given him for an eternal inheritance. ("His Spirit bears witness with our Spirit that we are the children of God.")

The Book of Revelation speaks of Christ's work of reconciling God's parallel Creations as follows:

> "I heard a great voice out of heaven saying, Behold, the Tabernacle of God, *the body of God's "true light,"* is with men, and he shall dwell with them, and they shall be his people, and God himself will dwell with them and be their God."

The "Arm of The Lord" God had imparted to man some four thousand years earlier was thus recognized as the light that appeared at Creation's inception. Indeed, the Life that was in that light was now revealed to mankind as "the true light that lights every man coming into the world." Therefore, those who enter into that light become children of the light. Collectively, they constitute "The Father's only begotten Son!" ("I go to prepare a place for you, that where I am there you may be also.")

JESUS

Having provided this overview of Christ's four-thousand-year labor, we can now consider his work within the confines of the days of Jesus.

When the temporal mind looks outward, what it sees is what it becomes – and what it sees is "worldly." It was not so with Jesus. When he looked outward he reconciled what he saw to himself, and what he saw was "spiritual." He saw life as a parallelism, a comparable, an image and likeness of his true Self, a mirror wherein he could behold his Spirit as in a glass. As the Word made flesh, his ministry became one of mirroring the mind's forthcoming spiritual transformation, a paralleling of events that would enhance mankind's level of comprehension. Therein, his labors opened the door to the kingdom of heaven.

It is impossible to understand the depths of Christ's work until we share in the adoptive process. We can read about his ministry of reconciliation, we can listen to others who teach life's spiritual principles, we can even attend the seminary of our choice and graduate with a Bachelor of Divinity degree and never obtain Christ's spiritual light. As he chided the Jews, "You search the Scriptures, for in them you think you have life, and their words testify of me; but you will not come to me, *you will not come to my light,* that you might have Life." We cannot know Christ by standing outside and looking in. The Creator's inner and outer worlds must spiritually communicate with each other. ("Why stands the weary traveler outside when all the temple is prepared within?")

To convey this spiritual reformation, Christ demonstrated the principle of obtaining UNITY through reconciliation, of "rightly dividing the Word of truth." But his success was limited. He repeated the words of Isaiah when he said, "Seeing, they see not, and hearing, they hear not; but if they will see with their eyes and hear with their ears and convert, I will heal them." Do not be misled. "Belief" alone is nothing. The mind "believes" what it fails to understand. The spirit of reconciliation is everything. When Jesus symbolically changed the water into wine, *the quasi-spiritual into the spiritual,* at the marriage in Canaan, his mother told the wine stewards, "Whatever he tells you to do, DO IT." She speaks to us all. Like the wine stewards, we too must follow his instructions. There is no other way. Only then will man's spirit be changed and healed.

In keeping with the external and internal witnesses of Scripture's Word, Jesus taught that "two witnesses" were necessary to fulfill the law of Life, as seen in the translating of quasi-spiritual symbolism into spiritual symbolism. He therefore sent his disciples into the countryside "two by two." They sowed the seed of God's redemptive truth throughout the land, and what they sowed was returned to them a thousandfold. By following Christ's instruction, they became "the first fruits" of the kingdom of heaven; and by extending their witness beyond the confines of Jerusalem, God's living presence within the human frame was communicated to all mankind.

Christ's ministry centered upon spiritually feeding the multitude and healing their misconceptions of life's content ("As the heavens are higher than the earth, so are my ways higher than your ways and my thoughts higher than your thoughts, said the Lord"), and his miracles demonstrated the healing of those errors. Scripture uses metaphors such as blind, deaf, lame, desolate and dead to describe the condition of the human psyche. Since "God is no respecter of persons," those metaphors apply to all. ("There is none righteous; no, not one.") It has therefore been said, "The moment of my birth was the moment of my death." But this wording has a double meaning. There is a first and second birth, and there is a first and second death. The first birth and death are experienced when we enter the temporal world. The second birth and death are experienced when we enter the spiritual world. But, "He that overcomes, *the first death*, shall not be hurt of the second death." In him, "Old things pass away, all things become new."

When Christ came teaching, "You shall know the truth and the truth shall make you free," he referred to the freedom that comes with the mind's release from temporal death. So, at his "second appearing," he heals the temporal and quasi-spiritual sick. He makes their blind to see and their deaf to hear, their lame to walk and their dead to rise. In this, he performs the greatest miracle of all: THE MIRACLE OF HEALING MAN'S SPIRIT. Upon receiving the mind of Christ, the psyche then beholds its "true light" and judges right judgment.

When Christ stood before Pilate in the Hall of Judgment and was asked, "Are you the king of the Jews?" he replied, "To this end was I born and for this cause came I into the world: that I should bear witness to the truth." As the Father had witnessed to his inner truth through created form, so had he given to the Son of man to witness to his inner truth through created form. In all things, Christ's ministry was a parallelism. ("I do only those things I see with the Father.") A friend once told me, "The gift of God is the gift of God." That is true. But to freely receive that gift we must, in turn, freely give of ourselves. ("Freely have you received, freely give.") Knowing this, Christ gave of all he had received from the Father. He was faithful, even unto death, and for his faithfulness he received a crown of Life. He therefore instructed his disciples, "The things that I do you shall do also"; and this we can do only by responding to the call: "FOLLOW ME!" ("I am the Way.")

19

Of Men and Angels

"He shall send forth his angels with a great sound of trumpet, *with great declarations of truth*, and gather his spiritual ones together, from one end of heaven to the other."

MATTHEW 24:31

The question is often asked, "What is life all about?" The answer is obvious. It is about judgment. ("All the ways of God are judgment.") Fundamentally, it is about a primal Spirit in search of its true identity; a Spirit that realizes that in order to become Self knowledgeable it must have a "second witness." To that end, the Creator became the created and God's "radiant light" appeared within Creation; and with the "formalizing" of that light, the Creator began to obtain Self-judgment.

But there were complications. He quickly discovered that creation embodied two forms of judgment. The first judgment witnessed to his dark experience within the void. The second judgment witnessed to the "true light" that appeared beyond the void. The Creator was thus confronted with a new challenge: to relate the diverse nature of these "two witnesses" to himself. He began by dividing his light from the darkness.

Since man was formed as a microcosm of the whole, we have only to look within ourselves to discover the psyche's inherent relationship to God. As we have seen, man's identity is determined by his knowledge, and that knowledge consists of a myriad number of lights. Collectively, those lights characterize the psyche. The same principle applies to God. The "radiant lights" within outpictured form represent the Creator's knowledge, and that knowledge constitutes his identity. Collectively, Creation's lights comprise his Spirit. Though Creation's form and man's form differ in appearance, both adhere to the same "pattern"; both are the "image and likeness" of God's person. His light is their light, his darkness is their darkness and his knowledge is their knowledge. ("You have no power whatsoever, except that given to you by the Father.") Upon recognizing this parallelism, the authors of Scripture characterized God as the indwelling "Father of lights."

With the placing of these reciprocal lights within the Creator's work, a "host body" was formed – a "host" that embodied the Creator's knowledge. The cosmos was thus perceived as "a multitude of the heavenly host." Yet, when viewed in microcosm, each light constituted a "host body." In keeping with that relationship, God was expressed as "the Lord of hosts."

Reflecting the Creator's intent to bring forth after his own kind, the cosmos' governing principle dictated that everything he had made bring forth after its own kind. Creation's "radiant light," *the Tree of Life*, in the midst of his work thus became commensurate to his Spirit. ("He is before all things and by him all things consist.") "The Lord of hosts" therefore appeared in the midst of his labors as "the Lord of spiritual lights." As the book of Hebrews relates, "He makes his angels, *his thoughts,* spirits; his ministers a flame of fire, *a host of enlightening truths.*" Creation's witnessing angels, *its "radiant lights,"* are thus identified as "finite spirits." Yet, collectively, they are infinite. Sequentially, this arrangement is characterized as follows:

- The Author of Creation's multitude of "radiant lights" is identified as "the Father of lights."
- The Creator of that "host of lights" is identified as "the Lord of hosts."
- That "radiant host" is subsequently identified as "a multitude of the heavenly host."
- The Creator's "heavenly host" is then characterized as "angels from on high."
- As "angels from on high," Creation's "radiant lights" are perceived as finite replicas of God's Spirit. Collectively, they disclose the character and glory of their Creator, the fullness of the Godhead, bodily.

Importantly, when God created "Adam," he committed Creation's "radiant light" to his keeping. This meant Creation's "angelic host" would witness not only to God, but also to the Christ within man. ("Upon bringing the first begotten into the world he said, Let all the angels of God, *all of Creation's radiant lights,* witness to him.") When Christ was questioned concerning man's resurrection he confirmed this

angelic relationship, saying: "The children of the resurrection, *those who have entered into eternal truth,*
neither marry nor are they given in marriage. Neither
can they die anymore; for they are equal to the angels,
the radiant truths, of heaven." Understandably, then, in
the resurrection, *in life eternal,* there is no division
between Father and Son. The Father's angels are the
Son's angels. The Father's light is the Son's light. The
Father's Spirit is the Son's Spirit. ("Father, glorify your
Son with your own self; with the glory which he had
with you before the world was.") Based upon this unity,
the Son of man comes in the clouds of heaven, *comes in
veiled form,* bringing all the holy angels with him.

When Adam was embodied as "the brightness of
God's glory and the express image of his person," all the
Father of lights had made received an audible voice.
Through that voice, "the host of heaven" obtained
audible expression. As God's living Word, man thus
became "the secret dwelling place of angels; the tabernacles of the Most High." Paul called God's radiant
Word in man "the secret that was kept from the foundation of the world: Christ in us, *heaven's angelic host
in man,* the hope of glory." However, the Father's
express purpose in creating man was to provide a
vehicle for the resolution of Creation's two forms of
judgment, the division of which appeared when Adam
and Eve ate of the Tree of Knowledge of good and evil.
For, as expressed in that simile, after responding to the
serpent's dark counsel they were deprived of knowing
the Creator's "radiant light," *the Christ that resided in
the midst of the Garden of God.*

Although Christianity depicts man as "saved" or
"lost," all is a work in progress. To define him as "a

fallen angel" reveals the psyche's shortsightedness. Man is definitely not a singular entity. ("Ten thousand times ten thousand ministered to him.") Clearly, the cosmos is more than one light. Like the mind, the heavens consist of an infinite number of lights. These lights must be reconciled to their Creator one at a time, experienced within the psyche as the conversion of one thought at a time. In judging these lights we judge angels ("Do you not know you are to judge angels?"), and through their conversion, *their pass-over,* what first appeared as darkness within Creation is unveiled and welcomed into God's eternal circle of light.

The wonder of this arrangement is that with the passage of angels from darkness into light, the mind's reality is changed. The Father confirms his presence within the angels, and the division between the two is removed. Consequently, when the mind beholds the Father's face it sees its true reflection, the one witnessing to the other. ("The angels that kept not their true light but left their habitations has he reserved in darkness unto the day of judgment.")

Since knowledge is comprised of lights that determine the mind's identity, the conversion of heaven's angels introduces man to "a new name" ("upon him that overcomes I will write my new name, *my NEW KNOWLEDGE*"); and that name is characterized as "the Sons of God." ("As many as are born of the Spirit of God, *the angels of God,* they are the Sons of God.") Thus, upon ascending into heaven, the Son of man brings all the holy angels, *all the knowledge of God,* with him. The book of Job characterizes heaven's angels as the Sons of God, and in that context Job is asked, "Where were you when the morning stars sang together and all the Sons of God shouted for joy?" Job gives no reply, but he should have asked, "Lord, was I not with you?"

The translating of the mind from temporal darkness into spiritual light is actively experienced when erroneous knowledge is recognized and spiritual truth rushes in to fill the void. The division separating the mind's temporal and spiritual viewpoints is then removed. Remember, all things must bring forth after their own kind. Temporal knowledge therefore brings forth temporal understanding and spiritual knowledge brings forth spiritual understanding. ("That born of the flesh is flesh and that born of the Spirit is Spirit.") Since God is the Father of lights, *the Lord of hosts,* all that is truly spiritual witnesses to him. We therefore know that if the symbolism fails to conform to the God-Principle, it is not spiritual. ("Any spirit that fails to confess that the Word of the Lord has come in the flesh is not of God.")

Typically, when Elisha saw Elijah taken up into heaven he witnessed: "My Father! My Father! The Chariot of Israel and the horsemen thereof." He saw the Chariot of Israel as God's spiritual instruction, and the angels who conveyed his light, *in the form of "signs and wonders,"* as the horsemen thereof. So, by recognizing the symbolism that accompanied Elijah's translation, Elisha obtained a "double portion" of Elijah's spirit. ("Be TRANSLATED by the renewing of your mind.") It is worth noting that the simile of Elijah's translation into heaven reflects the simile of Jacob's dream, in which he saw a ladder that reached all the way to heaven with the angels ascending and descending upon its steps. Both are analogies that relate to the mind's spiritual ascent through translation.

Because the Bible is a history of man's efforts to resolve the issues of darkness and light, it was inevitable that "the powers of darkness" should appear as warring against "the powers of light." John's Revelation symbolically expresses those conflicting forces when he reports:

"And there was war in heaven, *war within the mind.* Michael and his angels, *the angels of light,* fought against Satan and his angels, *the angels of darkness.*

And Satan and his angels, *the angels of darkness,* prevailed not; neither was their place found anymore in heaven.

And he that deceived the whole world, *the Prince of Darkness,* was cast out of heaven into the earth; and his angels were cast out with him."

Many of Scripture's similitudes depict the "warring of angels," but too often this form of symbolism falls upon its own sword. Appealing to the mind's passions and fears, it creates further division. Teaching the "wrath of God" has falsely led the mind to believe in doctrines of "purgatory," "hell fire," and "eternal damnation." ("Broad is the gate that leads to destruction; and many there are who go that way.") True spirituality is built upon higher ground. For that reason, we are called to a ministry of "forgiveness" and "reconciliation." The HIGH-WAY to heaven is ours to travel, but to successfully complete the journey we must be willing to forgive the angels of darkness that reside within the mind, and labor to bring them into God's light. In that day, "The Father of lights shall call them his people who were not his people; and his beloved who was not loved."

20

Bright Lights in Dark Places

> "A lamp is not brought forth to be hidden under a bushel; but to be set upon a lamp stand so that all who are in the house may see."
>
> MATTHEW 5:15

How do you tell a world steeped in religious belief that it is caught in a thicket of doctrinal misconceptions that must be sacrificed? ("You make the word of God of non-effect by your traditions.") How do you convince a person that their "chosen faith" is dead when they are convinced it is alive and well? ("While there are divisions among you are you not yet carnal and walk as men?") Christ warned the Jews of their error, but they did not believe him. Paul faced the same dilemma when he said, "I could wish myself accursed for Israel's sake!"

Today, both Jew and Christian attend the Synagogue or church of their choice, which is equivalent to supporting the truth of their choice, and they believe they do God's service. Without forethought, all are convinced they have chosen the right path and their "faith" will be vindicated. What has gone wrong? How did this colossal miscalculation occur? Having failed to recognize God's "true light," they have judged without a "second witness," and without this "second witness" they are void of true judgment. Consequently, their "faith" in God is dead. They are "the dead in Christ." They have "believed" in THE DELIVERER but have fallen short of being delivered.

In studying the Bible from an historic viewpoint, humanity's struggle with its own darkness becomes self-evident. At the other end of the spectrum, God is trying to bring light into the world but he is thwarted at every turn. His "signs and wonders" are continually misread, insomuch that by failing to comprehend his intentions, his light is transformed into "religious worship." The apostle refers to this temporal subversion when he writes, "Behold, Satan has transformed himself into an angel of light!" When Christ was observing Passover with his disciples in the upper room, *mirroring the Word's second reading,* he indicated the same, saying, "He that eats bread with me, *the quasi-spiritual mind,* has lifted up his heel against me." Although Judas was assigned the role of Christ's betrayer, more directly Christ's disclosure implicated the priestly hierarchy, for it was they who continually negated God's Word and sought his death.

On the other hand, Christ's warning that "a man's enemies are those of his own house," implicates us all, for "God is no respecter of persons." Knowing that Jew and Christian alike would misinterpret his spiritual instruction, he forewarned, "Many false teachers shall arise and deceive many; and because iniquity, *spiritual ineptness*, shall abound, the loves of many shall wax cold." He then continued: "Many shall come in my name, saying, I am the way. Go not after them, neither follow them; for as a great light that shines from east to west, so shall be the coming of the Son of man."

Using parables to convey man's deceptive religious practices, Christ exposed the inadequacy of "will worship" as follows:

"The kingdom of heaven, *as it pertains to the psyche*, is like unto ten virgins who took their lamps, *their knowledge*, and went into the night to meet their Lord. Five were wise, *spiritual*, and five were foolish, *quasi-spiritual*.

Those who were foolish took their lamps but took no additional oil, *no IN-SIGHT*, with them. But the wise provided additional oil for their lamps.

While their Lord tarried they all slumbered and slept; but at midnight they were awakened by the cry, Behold, your Lord is coming!

The ten virgins then arose and trimmed their lamps; and the foolish virgins said to the wise, Give us some of your oil, *some of your IN-SIGHT*, for our lamps, *our external lights*, have gone out.

But the wise answered, Not so! our oil will not serve the two of us. Go to those that provide for you and buy from them. And the foolish virgins went forth to purchase from those who buy and sell."

Note that the parable of the ten virgins leaves no room for reconciliation. That is because without spiritual enlightenment, reconciliation is impossible.

Compare the following parable to the one above and notice that while it differs in appearance, its truth remains the same.

"The kingdom of heaven, *as it pertains to the psyche,* is like a man that sowed good seed, *spiritual seed,* into his field, *into his knowledge.* But while men slept, an enemy, *the faculty of Reason,* came and sowed tares, *temporal seed,* among the wheat; and when the wheat, *the spiritual seed,* was sprung up the tares, *the temporal seed,* also appeared, *the mixing of the temporal tares with the spiritual wheat made the field quasi-spiritual.*

The laborers then came to their Lord and asked, Did you not sow good seed into your field? Who has sown these tares? The Lord replied, An enemy has done this.

Then the laborers asked, Should we go out and gather them up? No, he answered, for in rooting up the tares you may also harm the wheat. Let both grow

> together, *as a quasi-spiritual field,* until
> the harvest. Then I shall say to the
> reapers, Gather the tares into bundles
> and burn them; but gather the wheat
> into my barn."

Until we understand that God's Word has a first and second reading, *a linear and a parallel reading,* the mind will remain in darkness. Because religious "Orthodoxy" employs temporal knowledge to interpret spiritual truth, all of God's work is wrought with division; with contentions that confound his revelation and make his work of non-effect. ("Then shall that wicked one be discovered; who sits himself in the temple of God saying that he is God.") Nevertheless, all of the Creator's outpictured work, in its unadulterated state, remains intact. ("There is none lost but the son of perdition.")

The fundamental difference between the Word's first reading, *its quasi-spiritual form,* and its second reading, *its spiritual form,* is that its first reading witnesses to God's Spirit externally, *in a linear manner,* while its second reading witnesses to his Spirit internally, *in a parallel manner.* Once the Word's second reading is recognized, their two forms are reconciled and the misconception of the external reading is removed. The parable of the prodigal son reflects this accomplishment:

> "There was a man that had two sons, *the first was quasi-spiritual, the second was spiritual.* After receiving their inheritance,

the firstborn ventured into a foreign land, *temporal thought*, where he wasted his substance on riotous living. Meanwhile, the second-born remained at home with his father.

After wasting his inheritance and becoming destitute, the firstborn fearfully returned to the father's house ... repenting. Upon his arrival, his father went out to meet him and to forgive him for the error of his ways.

He then instructed his servants, *his angels*, to prepare a great feast to celebrate his son's return; for the father said, This is my son who was dead and is alive again; he was lost and is found.

All who resided within the father's house then came to the feast and, together, they rejoiced."

It is difficult but necessary to recognize that religion, in all forms, is an outpicturing of the mind's temporal concept of spirituality. When Jesus told Nicodemus, "You must be born again or you cannot see the kingdom of God," he implied that the whole of the world's religious community was estranged from God's truth – for Nicodemus was a typical example of mankind's failure to recognize the spiritual aspect of the Creator's work. Having transformed his revelatory instruction into religious practices, both the mind and its chosen method of worship needed to be "born again." Know of a certainty that many of man's "holy practices" are definitely "unholy."

They are not of God. They are the product of man's corrupt faculty of "Reason." ("We fight not against flesh and blood, but against powers and principalities and spiritual wickedness in high places.")

Because temporal "will worship" denied God's true light, Christ became known as "the lamb of God, *the light of God,* that was slain, *that suffered death,* from the foundation of the world." We have only to examine history to validate that truth. Genesis emphasizes the same when God warns Adam that if he eats of the Tree of Knowledge of good and evil, he will surely die. When the first couple refutes that warning they succumb to division and God's Word in man dies; it becomes of non-effect. Thereafter, until the time of Christ's resurrection, the world is plagued by a state of living death. However, with the Word's regeneration God's "true light" finally emerged from darkness, revealing a way of spiritual Passover. ("I have longed to eat this Passover with you.") Today the dead in Christ, who hear his voice, are passed from death unto Life. John's Book of Revelation therefore characterizes Christ as, "He that was dead and is alive forevermore and has the keys of death and hell."

When humanity's spiritual progress is reviewed in the light of history, it is evident that man's perception of "life after death" needs to change. For until that change is made, his promised "eternal glory" cannot come to fruition. Consider the following:

- When God gathered Moses unto himself, Israel entered the Promised Land.
- When God gathered Elijah unto himself, the Son of man appeared in the prophets.

- When God gathered John the Baptist – the last of the prophets – unto himself, the Son of God appeared in Jesus Christ.
- When God gathered Jesus Christ unto himself, the Holy Ghost was given, signaling Christ's return in the glory of his Father.

As illustrated, a "second death" became the prerequisite to an expanded life. As Jesus told his disciples, "I have power to lay down my life; and I have power to take it up again." That power is given to all who come "IN THE NAME OF THE LORD." ("He shall be blest who comes in the name of the Lord.")

Clearly, there are bright lights shining in dark places that mankind has never seen. ("There shall be no night there; for the Lord God gives them light.") Knowing this, we should not repeat Israel's mistake at Sinai when the people said, "Let us not look upon the face of God or we shall surely die." Rather, we should choose the path least trodden; we should bury our dead and move on. For, "If we are buried in the likeness of Christ's death, we shall appear with him in the likeness of his resurrection." The Book of Revelation therefore counsels, "Be faithful unto death and I will give you a crown of Life."

21

Continuous Whole

"Lord, you are very great; you are clothed with honor and majesty. You have covered yourself with light as with a garment. You have stretched out the heavens like a curtain and walked upon the wings of the wind. You have laid the beams of your chambers in the waters and prepared the foundations of the earth that they should not be removed."

PSALMS 104:1-6

Will life on earth always be limited to man's temporal experience? Will it continue to be fractured and fragmented? Or can it become orderly and progressive? The answer depends upon our ability to embrace change. For sure, that born of temporal knowledge witnesses to things appearing in the temporal world, and that born of spiritual knowledge witnesses to things appearing in the spiritual world. By contrast, man's tumultuous history spans thousands of *linear* years; yet, "To the Lord, a day, *in paralleling,* is like a thousand years." The answer, then, depends upon changing our concept of God and his universe. We must cease from knowing "in part" and acting "in part." We must recognize that life, with its countless facets, belongs to THE CONTINUOUS WHOLE. Only then shall we find peace.

Today's religious leaders are fully aware that humanity's present quasi-spiritual course will never lead to a spiritualized world. But how can this age-old dilemma be resolved? Only by awakening to a new concept of God's eternal truth. ("You shall know the truth and the truth shall make you free.") And our wake-up call to that truth begins with recognizing that God's voidal experience mirrors our own.

What appeared in the beginning with God was also predestined for man. ("Let us make man in our image and after our likeness.") The eternal pattern was established when the light of God's Spirit filled the abyss but failed to comprehend its own image and likeness. ("My light shall go forth and make the crooked places straight; and we shall share the treasures of darkness.") This "common point of origin" was first recognized when Moses was instructed to make all things after the pattern, *the pattern of God's image and likeness in man,* revealed to him on the mount. In keeping with that pattern, the initial tenet established between God and man became "personal darkness," and thereafter their common desire to obtain spiritual light. The first step taken in that direction came when God, and later man, looked inward and examined the "light of Life" that issued from within their beings. And what they saw they outpictured, saying, "Let there be light!" And, in turn, each saw that their "true light" was good.

Because the Creator's primal light was conceived in darkness, mankind's first knowledge likewise appeared as "a light shining in a dark place." As parallelisms, formal Creation signified God's primal state and temporal knowledge signified man's primal state. Their mutual task became one of dividing their "true light" from the dark anomaly that enveloped the whole world, and that task was first initiated when God divided his light from the darkness. Mirroring that transitional event, mankind's first spiritual enlightenment commenced with God providing revelatory "signs and wonders" to divide his light from the darkness. Self-revelation thus became the common objective of God, of his Christ and of man. All three sought to free them-selves from darkness. All three sought spiritual fulfill-ment through knowing their "true light." ("Whatever the Father does, the Son does likewise.")

Admittedly, this format conflicts with traditional religious doctrine. Nonetheless, as the Father's plan had called for reconciling outer darkness through the use of his "true light," so the Son's plan called for reconciling outer darkness through the use of his "true light." Once their mutual labors came to fruition, the Son of man would then share in all facets of the Creator's work. ("The Father and I are one.") Regrettably, when religious doctrine excludes itself from participating in THE CONTINUOUS WHOLE, it excludes mankind also. In his book, *The Rubaiyat*, Omar Khayyam sums up man's inclusion in "the continuous whole" of God's work as follows:

"With earth's first clay they did the last man knead. And there, of the last harvest, sowed the seed.

And the first morning of creation wrote what the last dawn of reckoning shall read."

When the disciple, John, recognized that man was the recipient of all God had made, he affirmed, "The true light that lights every man coming into the world is that light which appeared in the beginning with God." He saw no conflict in saying that man, in order to be "one" with the Spirit of God, had to share all things in common with God. ("All that the Father has are mine, and all mine are the Father's.") Because Christ's disciples initially failed to understand the concept of one God in all, Jesus said, "Where I go you cannot now come; but, afterwards, *when the Son of man comes in his Father's glory,* you shall follow."

In drawing comparisons between man's "voidal experience" and God's "voidal experience," we should note that the same principles used to express man's salvation are also applicable to God's salvation. For instance, when the Creator outpictured his Spirit into formal substance, he did the following:

- He committed himself to CONVERSION, translating all that was his into formal Creation.
- He committed himself to REBIRTH, commanding all that was his to be "born again."

- He committed himself to REFORMATION, submitting all that was his to be formed anew.
- He committed himself to RENEWAL, expressing Creation as a RE-KNOWING of his Spirit.
- He committed himself to PASSOVER, providing a way wherein darkness would be swallowed up with light.
- He committed himself to RESURRECTION, allowing all that was his to behold his glory.

The only difference between the translating of God's glory into Creation and the translating of Christ's glory into man is that the first converts the invisible into the visible, *spiritual evolution,* while the second converts the visible into the invisible, *spiritual involution.* As Christ said, "I came out from the Father, now I return to the Father."

This brings us to one of the most startling revelations the Bible offers. What did Jesus envision for himself and man when he said, "Father, glorify your Son with your own self; with the glory that he had with you before the world was." This prompts the question: If there was only spirit and void in the beginning ("Before the world was."), wherein was the glory? And, if God's glory in the dark abyss was greater than his glory in Creation, what moved him to create something that lessened his glory? Also, this conflicts with the prophet's vision, when he says, "The glory of this latter house shall be greater than the former." There is a logical explanation, but we must look beyond appearances.

As previously shown, God's Self revelation and man's Self revelation are complementary. Each seeks to know their own truth through similes that express their glory. Accordingly, what God outpictured into form was a reflection of what appeared within him. In that context, form is seen as mirroring the glory that was with the Father before the world was. So when Christ asked the Father to glorify his Son with the glory he shared with him before the world was, HE ASKED THAT HIS EXTERNAL GLORY BE INTERNALLY GLORI-FIED: THAT MAN BE GLORIFIED WITH THE OUTPIC-TURED GLORY THAT SIGNIFIED THE CREATOR'S TRUE LIGHT. This signaled the approaching resolution of the quasi-spiritual darkness that appeared within the world from its inception. ("Those who are well need not a physician, but those who are sick.") Therein, all would be reconciled to the Father; all that identified with Creation's "radiant light" would share the glory they had with the Father before the world was.

The apostle speaks of the Son's entry into this ever-lasting state as "the glory that excelleth." The following examples depict the same:

- "No man has ascended into the Father's glory, *into heaven's light,* except he that came down from heaven; even the Son of man who is in heaven's light."
- "Heaven and earth are full of the glory of the Lord, *the radiant light of the Lord.*"
- "The kingdom of God, *the light of God,* is within you; the kingdom of heaven, *the glory of heaven,* is among you."

○ "Walk in his light, *ADOPT THE LIGHT,* that you might be the children of the light."
○ "The glory of the Lord, *the light of the Lord,* filled the house."
○ "Come, beloved of my Father, and inherit the glory, *the light,* that was prepared for you from the foundation of the world."

After Christ had finished witnessing to the revelation the Father had given him, he was glorified with the Father's eternal glory. ("I go unto the Father.") Through his witness, the path to enlightenment was made available to all who would commit to his "Way." ("Your Word, O Lord, is a light unto my path, a lamp unto my feet.") Today, to as many as conform to the pattern of Christ's revelation, the same are glorified with him in the light that was with the Father before the world was. ("As I overcame and am set down in my Father's throne, so to him that overcomes will I grant to sit with me in my throne.") God, and the Sons of God, are thus recognized as KNOWLEDGEABLE SPIRITS RESIDING IN THE MIDST OF A WITNESSING CREATION.

For countless generations, mankind has longed to dwell in a spiritualized world – but he has always looked upon his aspirations as belonging to another time. ("I shall see him, but not now. I shall behold him, but not nigh.") Limited by the scope of his vision, man has failed to grasp the age-old truth that, through Christ, he is grafted into THE CONTINUOUS WHOLE of God's work. Perhaps now, after so long a time, the darkness that has plagued his days shall pass.

"He was in the world, and the world was made by him, but the world knew him not. He came unto his own and his own received him not.

BUT TO AS MANY AS DID RECEIVE HIM, TO THEM GAVE HE THE POWER TO BECOME THE SONS OF GOD."

Epilogue

Having read through *The Book of Lights – Unveiling the Mystery of God,* the reader should be aware that the Bible is expressly designed to reveal the various levels of comprehension and reality available to mankind. Since those levels of cognizance apply to everyone, the following summary is provided to give the reader an opportunity to evaluate their spiritual progress and assess their current understanding of God and the world we live in. ("Then shall I know, even as I am known.")

As an analogy, the Bible relates to mankind as a four-dimensional body of light. Two readings witness to his reality in the below, *the temporal mind and the quasi-spiritual mind,* and two readings witness to his reality in the above, *the spiritual mind of Christ and the spiritual mind of God.* These four dimensions unfold before the reader as SELF-CHARACTERIZING INSIGHTS. Since God's work is progressive, the ability of the reader to understand the Bible's spiritual content will be determined by their present level of reality.

To simplify these four inherent dimensions, this presentation has identified the Bible as having two readings; with each reading having "two witnesses." The first reading relates to the temporal world, the second reading relates to the spiritual world.

In the Bible's first reading, its "two witnesses" are aligned with man's linear perception of life. In the second reading, its "two witnesses" are aligned with man's parallel perceptions of life.

In concert with the Bible's first reading, all begins on a temporal or sensory level of understanding, creating a "first witness." That first witness then evolves, incrementally, into a moral or semispiritual, *religious,* state of reality, giving birth to a "second witness." These "two witnesses" are earthy and comprise the mind's two initial levels of comprehension. In the Bible's second reading, life is revealed as an all-inclusive spiritual parallelism. Therein, the mind of man is reconciled to the mind of Christ and a spiritual "first witness" is provided. ("I would that they be where I am.") This "first witness" then evolves incrementally and at length culminates with Christ's ascent and glorification in the Father – *his glorification in the Holy Ghost* – giving birth to a "second witness."

Since, in the second reading, the mind of God, the mind of Christ and the mind of man are counted as "one," man ascends in the body of Christ and is glorified, with him, in the Father. ("Father, glorify your Son with your own self") God, Christ, Man and Creation at large thus emerge as one all-inclusive Spiritual body. ("He that overcomes shall inherit all things.") With the myriad facets of God's work converging to form a UNIVERSAL COLLECTIVE CONSCIOUSNESS, there is nothing lost but the mind's dark misconceptions.

Having laid this introspective foundation, we can now move forward and continue our exploration of Christ's spiritual work as presented in *The Book of Lights II – Unveiling the Mystery of Christ.*

Index

B

belief, 8, 13, 128, 129, 165
beliefs, 9, 19, 135, 143

C

Christ, 22, 27, 65, 95, 149, 159, 177

E

enlightened, 8
enlighten, 46
enlightening, 30, 159
enlightenment, 15, 175, 179

J

judgment, 24, 44, 105, 106, 160
first judgment, 23, 24, 157
last judgment, 24, 25, 45, 144
right judgment, 7, 154

L

linear, 22, 23, 25, 47, 55, 128

M

manifest, 50
manifestation, 16, 50, 66, 79, 105, 150
manifesting, 22, 51

O
outpicture, 105
   outpictured, 31, 47, 50, 127, 141, 158, 176, 178
   outpicturing, 52, 67, 115, 170

P
parallel, 22, 45, 55
   paralleling, 46, 140
   parallelism, 25, 54, 152
Passover, 75, 91, 166, 171
   pass-over, 161
principle, 37, 54, 73, 105, 135, 148
   principles, 126, 152

Q
quasi-spiritual, 15, 21, 55, 88, 101, 169
quickened, 39, 40
   quickening, 26, 28, 126, 127, 142, 150

R
reason, 44, 45, 46, 51, 75, 97, 171
   reasoned, 116
   sensory reason, 32
reconcile, 31, 35, 136
   reconciled, 22, 84, 152, 161, 169, 178
   reconciliation, 89, 134, 152, 153, 163
   reconciling, 32, 59, 144, 151, 175
resurrection, 24, 123, 138, 143, 159

S
similitude, 61
   similitudes, 87, 117, 163
symbol, 60, 68, 79, 111, 120, 123

Book Order Form

For additional copies of *The Book of Lights – Unveiling the Mystery of God* please order via the following:

Fax Orders: 586-558-9791. Send this form with order.
Telephone Orders: 586-573-3077
E-mail Orders: pandp_publishing@comcast.net
Postal Orders: P & P Publishing
P.O. Box 1051, Warren, Michigan 48090 U.S.A.

Your Name: _____

Address: _____

City and State:_____

Zip:_____ Phone #: _____

Please send me _____ copies at $14.95 ea. (U.S Funds)
(Call for discounts on orders over 2 books)
Total price of copies to be sent $_____
Add 6% sales tax (MI residents only) $_____
Add $2.00 per book, for shipping/handling $_____
Add $2.00 per book if you want Priority Mail $_____
                                               Total $_____

Payment: Check _____   Credit Card: VISA _____
                                                              MasterCard _____

Credit card number:

_____

Cardholder name:

_____

Expiration date:

_____

Cardholder's Signature:

_____

visit us at truelightbooks.com